Contents

Front cover picture: Standing in a displacement camp in Khartoum,
a girl displays a drape celebrating the heroes of the Church in Sudan.
(Photograph: Andrzej Polec)

Cardinal Gabriel Zubeir Wako
Archbishop of Khartoum

Preface

"Despite all the actions taken against us and the persecution of so many innocent people, the spirit of God is alive in our country; the Church is growing just like the first Christian communities. In the middle of it all is our Cardinal – our Cardinal is great; he is active; he is just like a father with his children. That is my impression. He is a man of great faith, someone with a great love for his people and for the Church. He wants the Church in the Sudan to grow."

These words spoken in Khartoum by Sister Grace, a newly professed nun, are typical of what I and others have heard on project trips to Sudan undertaken by staff and co-workers of the charity Aid to the Church in Need.

In the face of so much suffering, Cardinal Gabriel Zubeir Wako is an inspiration to a people who struggle for religious and cultural freedom in one of the world's most oppressive and cruel environments.

A writer of simple, yet disturbingly profound truth, Cardinal Zubeir Wako's poems and letters are an astonishing testimony to faith under fire.

Taken from the Archdiocese of Khartoum publication *God's Love*, and subsequent pamphlets, *Roll Back the Stone of Fear* reveals the truth about a people who have suffered in silence for far too long.

My thanks must go to Cardinal Zubeir for giving permission to reproduce his writings, to Fr Martin Saturlino Adele, his secretary, and to Tony Smith and other staff at Aid to the Church in Need (UK) for their help in bringing this book to fruition.

John Pontifex
Head of Press & Information
Aid to the Church in Need (UK)

Introduction
An Appreciation of Cardinal Gabriel Zubeir Wako
by Bishop Daniel Adwok Marko Kur
Auxiliary Bishop of Khartoum

When the announcement came in 2003 that Archbishop Zubeir Wako was to be made a Cardinal, the immediate reaction of the people was that of joy. People finally understood the place of the Church in the Christian community and in the world. At last people saw in the Archbishop a leader in the midst of his people. Many people felt it was the summit of so many years of struggle to affirm the dignity of the Christian citizens of the country. The Church in Sudan has grown so much over the past 30 years. Not long ago, the Church consisted of small numbers of Christian communities spread out mainly in the south of the country. Now there are millions of Christians all over the country. The Church has grown despite the fact that our situation has not been easy. Instead we have grown despite the struggle with the government and the struggle with war.

The Cardinal has personally built up the confidence of the Christian community, especially the displaced people in the north of the country. The Cardinal is a man who is not afraid. His trust in God is very, very great. You could say that his aim as a pastor is to reassure the Christian community that the compassion of God is with them even in the worst moments of their suffering. His whole ministry is built around the compassion of God towards the individual and the family. He wants them to know that God will not disappoint them.

The Cardinal conducts his ministry on a level, which is realistic. He wants to find ways that will actually deliver pastoral ministry - that it will actually reach those who need it. This is clear in the Synods he has organised in the Church. We are now in the Second Synod.

Cardinal Zubeir is always the same; he wants to find the right pastoral situation in which the people - especially those most in need - can hear the Gospel.

He is always looking to the future; he is a man with a vision for the Church; a vision for the family; a vision for the north of the Sudan, a vision for the different programmes in the Archdiocese. He wants every pastoral agent to have vision - the priests, the religious, the catechists and the lay people. He does not just want people to work with a purpose to get through today's work. He wants them to have vision for the future, people who minister with their lives as well as their hands.

The Rt. Rev. Daniel Adwok, Auxiliary Bishop of Khartoum

Cardinal Zubeir's poems and pastoral letters are an essential part of his ministry. They are read out in churches and parish centres in the huge Archdiocese of Khartoum. Also, many thousands of copies of them are printed and distributed to the people. They take them home and read and re-read them. Part of why they are so important to the people is that they can see that the Cardinal realises only too well the difficult situation in which the displaced communities live. He identifies with them. His messages open the door of welcome to the man who is in trouble and has no hope, to those who are suffering and those who are imprisoned. He wants to restore hope in the light of the Gospel. What makes his writings so readable is his understanding of the people's situation. They think: 'Here is a person who is our leader, someone who has got the same heart as us, someone who faces the same suffering as us, someone who experiences the same pain as us'.

> The Cardinal's messages open the door of welcome to the man who is in trouble and who has no hope.

So far as the international community is concerned, the Cardinal's writings are a vital witness to the truth about what Christians in the Sudan have suffered and how the Church is ministering to them in their time of trial. People outside the Sudan, reading *Roll Back the Stone of Fear*, should remember that most Christians in Khartoum are living in displacement camps. His message to them is that their suffering is not the end of the road. There is a light at the end of the tunnel for them. He sets out to touch their hearts, especially in the midst of their suffering.

Through the media, the world knows about Darfur, the region in west Sudan where huge numbers of people were killed by militia fighters and many more fled for their lives. What happened in Darfur is a reflection of what happened in the south. And yet, in the midst of such suffering against the Christian people, you will not find in the Cardinal's writings a sermon of violence or hatred. I remember in particular one incident when a parish centre was destroyed and people there were very upset. We went over there and preached a message of hope; we told them not to fill their hearts with hatred. Hope is what liberates the people. Never does the Cardinal preach revenge. It is this message of hope, which I believe has helped so much to ease the conflict in the south of the country.

Cardinal Gabriel Zubeir Wako - A Brief Biography
by John Pontifex

It is hard, if not impossible, to imagine the scale of the trials and tribulations borne by the leader of the Catholic Church in Sudan. In the last 20 years alone, nearly three million have lost their lives as Sudan has ricocheted from one war to another. Since independence from Britain in 1956, Africa's largest country has enjoyed just 10 years of peace (1972-1982). In the last 20 years, up to five million have fled their homes to escape war and famine, giving Sudan the dubious honour of reportedly having the world's largest internally displaced population. Those who have succeeded in finding new homes face the constant threat of famine, disease and the day-to-day harassment from Sudanese militia and security forces.

In such circumstances, the task of restoring lost hope, of rekindling a faith all but destroyed, of seeking reconciliation and peace where only bitterness and misery abound, would seem nothing more than an impossible dream, a feat totally beyond human capability. And yet, over the course of 25 years as Archbishop of Khartoum, Gabriel Zubeir Wako, the man they call "Father Courage", has made these very aspirations his daily bread.

What kind of man could possibly set about this awesome challenge, and remain steadfast in pursuit of it for so long? What is it about his life story that prepared him for the hard and stony road ahead?

The future Cardinal Archbishop of Khartoum was born in Mboro, a small town in the Bahr el Ghazal region of southern Sudan. It is of no small importance that the district in which he grew up was to become one of the bloodiest theatres of war. In the Bahr el Ghazal region alone, up to one million people have died in the last 20 years.

Few if any signs of what was to come were apparent on 27th February 1941, when Gabriel Zubeir Wako was born. His parents, Placido Wako and his wife, Felicita Juno, were devout Catholics and inevitably the Faith was crucial to the future Cardinal's upbringing. Placido was a senior catechist in Wau, the county town of Bahr el Ghazal, and, Sunday by Sunday, the proud father would lead his children to church in single file.

A key turning point in the young Gabriel's journey towards priesthood came very early on. Attracted to the Church from a young age, he took to accompanying his parish priest as he walked around the town saying his breviary. The little boy would look out for the missionary, Father Angelo Arpe, waiting for him to pass the Wako family home. They would walk together and stop beside a pond where they sat on two large rocks. But the tranquillity came to an abrupt halt when Fr Angelo was assassinated. The murder came just hours after the the young Gabriel Zubeir Wako received his first Holy Communion.

In 1951, aged just 10, Gabriel Zubeir Wako entered the Minor Seminary in Bussere (Wau). His abilities soon came to the attention of his superiors. A priest, who taught the young Gabriel at the age of 15, said: "I have spent almost all my life teaching theology to students and I can confirm that I never found another student possessing the same degree of intelligence." As well as academic study, he excelled in music and was a leading figure in seminary initiatives to adapt sacred Latin liturgical texts to familiar settings of Sudanese tribal music. It prepared him well for the post-Vatican II years when the then Bishop Zubeir Wako oversaw changes in the liturgy to enable greater expression of African culture.

After completing his studies at St Paul's National Seminary in Yei, one of Sudan's most southerly towns, Gabriel Zubeir Wako was ordained priest on July 23, 1963. Aged just 22, he was so young to be ordained that he required a special dispensation from Rome. He would need all the vigour and enthusiasm of youth for the years ahead.

In 1964, General Ibrahim Abboud's military regime expelled 300 foreign missionaries from Sudan. In Wau diocese, clergy numbers haemorrhaged, falling to just six in a few short years. Initially appointed assistant priest in the town of Kuajok, Father Gabriel soon had to run the parish alone, when the parish priest, Fr Dal Maso, was expelled. In a very short time, he was also appointed district inspector of Christian Religious Education and when it became clear that his former junior seminary, St Anthony's in Bussere, faced closure because of shortage of priests, he stepped in

"O Lord hear my prayer":
School children at Jabal Auliya,
south of Khartoum.
Photo: A. Polec.

as rector. Years later, he would recall: "After my ordination, things became difficult. I found myself practically alone. We were only a handful of priests in the diocese, but we tried to keep things going despite our small number."

Life became tougher still for the young priest when Wau fell into the grip of the first civil war to erupt in Sudan, after the collapse of the government left by the British before independence in 1956. Looking back years later, Zubeir Wako said: "We were confined to Wau. One of us priests was killed. There were massacres and house arrests and some of us were on the hit list. A number of nights were passed under our beds. The morning after shoot-out was our first chance to see who was still alive."

These were years of tough pastoral experience. Lacking financial support, the future cardinal was close to the breadline and only had a bicycle for transport. Such experiences would mean he could look his priests in the eye when as Archbishop he would call on them to remain steadfast in faith dispite all the odds against them.

Father Gabriel's baptism of fire in the formative years of his priesthood ended in 1968 when he was sent to Rome for post-graduate study. Returning to Sudan in 1972, his life was once again a juggling act; he was appointed procurator for the Wau Vicariate, vicar delegate, provincial commissioner for the Scouts and Guides and once again rector of Wau's St Andrew's Seminary – posts he held simultaneously.

In 1975, Gabriel Zubeir Wako was named Bishop of Wau. He was just 34 years old. War had ravaged his people and morale was poor. The seminary he had worked so hard to build up was struggling – only six students were there. The continuing war severely hampered outreach to the people. One hope remained – the catechists. With priests in short supply, the catechists provided the backbone of many parishes and mission centres. The youthful bishop set to work improving the catechists' formation in scripture and liturgy.

But before much could be done, Bishop Zubeir Wako had to bid farewell to his home region. In 1979, he was appointed Archbishop of Khartoum. Still not yet 40, he had been handed what to many was a poisoned chalice. The 1972 Addis Ababa Peace Agreement, which ended Sudan's first civil war (1964–1972), was already under threat. By the time Zubeir Wako took over as Archbishop in 1981, the Numeiry regime was slipping out of control. Desperate for support to bolster his crumbling power base, Numeiry brokered a deal with Islamic hard-liners and in September 1983 the much feared strict Muslim Shari'a law was introduced. Tension was compounded by the discovery of oil in southern Sudan. Relations between the Government and the southern rebels broke down with both sides claiming rights to the oil. But by then, the civil war, in which so many were to lose their lives, had begun its deadly course.

The Church, meanwhile, was not without problems of its own. The Archbishop later recalled: "I found myself to be the only native Sudanese priest among the diocesan clergy." With the outbreak of civil war, the stream of internal refugees heading north to Khartoum and beyond soon became a flood. They were a people who had lost everything. A diocesan account of the time gave this verdict: "Many people have become so weak that they are incapable of reacting to abuses against them and their rights. The physical, emotional and spiritual sufferings of many Sudanese are untold."

From day one, Archbishop Zubeir Wako was a shepherd devoted to the pursuit of peace - but never at the expense of justice. He set about developing a pastoral vision through patient listening, consulting, co-ordinating and planning with his co-workers, priests, religious and lay people. The first fruits of his search for united and pastoral co-operation and cohesion came with the Archdiocesan Synod (1987-1991). "The Church God wants us to be", the document enshrining the synod, became for all pastoral workers the *Magna Carta* of the Archdiocese.

Archbishop Zubeir Wako threw himself into the task of inspiring the faithful to be true witnesses to Christ come what may. Everybody was challenged to play their part; the Youth Chaplaincy, the Justice and Peace Committee; the message was plain for all to see in the formation of catechists, the care of seminarians, the on-going formation of priests and religious and the dignity of women within the Church. Each programme set out to renew hope and purpose among a people increasingly disenfranchised by a government ever-stiffening in its militant resolve.

Youngsters revising for an exam at a "Save the Saveable" School in Mayo displacement camp, Khartoum.

Calls on the Church to play a greater role in society in Khartoum became increasingly urgent as torrents of Christians fled into the city to escape the bitter civil war being waged in the south. Hundreds of thousands sought sanctuary in the capital only to become victims of yet more violence. By the early 1990s, the Bashir government had lost its patience with the influx of southerners and ruthlessly began bulldozing their homes and driving them out of the city centre. They were forced to live in displacement camps often lacking the most basic of needs - water, food, sanitation and health care. Many were faced with starvation and disease.

Archbishop Zubeir Wako responded with a ground-breaking initiative, which was to become the project "dearest to my heart", as he put it. "Save the Saveable", which started out as a sideline scheme for children of barely primary school age, quickly grew into a diocesan-wide programme of vital educational and social support. Shocked and dismayed by the desperate struggle of poverty-stricken Christian families trying to give their children a little education in the misery of the displacement camps, Archbishop Zubeir Wako started to organise Church schools. At first, only a few pre-school children took part in the scheme but, emboldened by the overwhelming show of support by clergy and lay alike, "Save the Saveable" soon spread throughout the displacement camps around Khartoum and further out into the neighbouring towns and villages. Central to the scheme was the provision of free food for the children and social support for families. The parents did not pay a penny - the diocese footed the bill, heavily reliant on help from aid agencies.

The initiative aroused the deepest suspicions of the Omar al Bashir government but, undaunted, Archbishop Zubeir Wako insisted upon the Christian population's right to their own education system, organised totally separate from the government schools, whose heavy emphasis on Islam doctrine inevitably discriminates against non-Muslims. At its peak, in 2000, almost 70,000 children were on the school roll. And yet, "Save the Saveable" was in many ways at its weakest when most successful. As more and more children took advantage of the free education and social care, "Save the Saveable"

A blessing for the people: The Cardinal at a displacement camp chapel. Photo: A. Polec.

was in the red to the tune of £500,000. Soon it was not just the Government who were of major concern to the Archbishop; the 1,500 teachers at the schools were demanding wages the Church could not pay. The situation deteriorated so far that the Archbishop feared his failure to pay the staff would end with his imprisonment. A fundraising campaign was mounted in 2004 by the Catholic charity, Aid to the Church in Need.

In autumn 2003 as the Archbishop's trials reached one of their bleakest moments, the clouds parted allowing two rays of glory to shine on the Church in Sudan. First came news of the long awaited canonisation of Daniel Comboni. Popularly hailed as the Father of the Sudanese Church, the 19th century missionary is remembered as the leading figure in the evangelisation of a pagan African people. The missionary order, which takes his name, built on Comboni's legendary work to expand the Christian presence in Sudan far and wide, especially in the south of the country.

Now a Cardinal, Archbishop Zubeir arrives back from Rome with Bishop Adwok (October 2003).

Comboni's canonisation coincided with the elevation of Archbishop Zubeir to the rank of Cardinal. The news caused shock and amazement throughout the Sudanese Church. Never before had Sudan been honoured with its own Cardinal, and that it should be a native Sudanese who received the red hat was an added source of pride.

That October day, when Cardinal Zubeir Wako's aeroplane touched down in Khartoum, the new Prince of the Church was welcomed by up to a million people. Row upon row of people lined the streets from the airport to the cathedral where he celebrated a Mass of thanksgiving. For him it was an emotional moment. But more than that; both events – the elevation of Zubeir Wako as Cardinal and the canonisation of Daniel Comboni – sent out a signal to the forces of oppression in Sudan that the Church was far from vanquished. Indeed, they demonstrated that the people's rock-like faith had stood firm through the most tempestuous of times to emerge as a beacon of hope not just for Sudan but for the world.

The theme of hope was to reach its climax on May 26th 2004 when the Government of Sudan finally signed a peace accord with the rebel Sudanese People's Liberation Army/Movement (SPLA/M). It was the closest the country had come to drawing a line under a 20-year civil war, which Cardinal Zubeir Wako so desperately sought to end.

The man from Wau's unique blend of unswerving determination, undisputed intelligence and contagious religious zeal has inspired a new generation of Sudanese Catholics. When he became Archbishop, the clergy numbered very few Sudanese within their ranks. Now with up to 20 priestly ordinations in Khartoum every year, it is the foreign missionaries who are in the minority in the Khartoum diocese. No more can the government claim that the Church in Sudan is made up of foreigners. A Church that numbered barely 900,000 in 1960, now counts up to four million baptised. In Khartoum, the influx of Christians from the South and the huge numbers of conversions has had a profound impact on the diocese. According to the latest figures, there are almost 950,000 Catholics in Khartoum diocese and every year about 5,000 adults are baptised after rigorous catechesis spanning up to three years. When Archbishop Zubeir Wako took over the Khartoum diocese in 1981 there were just four parishes – Masalma in Omdurman, Khartoum North, St Joseph's and SS Peter and Paul. Now, there are 29 parishes extending across Khartoum and into the pastoral region of Kosti, about 150 miles to the south of the capital. Numbers of priests in the diocese have grown to almost 80.

Cardinal Zubeir Wako has played no small part in this resurgence of a Church, constantly under attack from persecution. But his response to the slaughter of millions of innocents has not been to lead his people in self-righteous outrage. Rather, he has always been an advocate of reconciliation and forgiveness. Against all the odds, he has continued to be the still small voice of calm.

The year 2004 was not Sudan's first experience of mass bloodshed and misery. The Darfur crisis, in which militia killed thousands of people and a million and more fled their homes, is strikingly similar to the reign of terror, which pulverised the south of Sudan for so long. Only now, as the veil of silence is lifted over Darfur, is the truth about Sudan's suffering reaching the ears of the wider world. Perhaps only now will the international community begin to demand the peaceful resolution of conflict, which the Cardinal has always preached. Perhaps only now will the world find out why the Sudanese Christians still insist on calling their new Cardinal "Father Courage".

After Mass on Ash Wednesday. Photo: A. Polec.

I
Prayer-Poems

CHRISTMAS 1984

Ever Since
You, the Word, became flesh and lived among us
Conversation and relationships have become difficult.
For now,
There is no "I" without YOU, no "We" without YOU,
No "you" without YOU, no "he" or "she" without YOU,
No "they" without YOU,
But,
You have straightened things out:
I, we, you, he, she and they,
Can now all say: "Our Father".
We cannot change our Language,
But do help us to change our relationships
Into one universal "WE"
Because of that one "Our Father":
And the one YOU living among us.

EASTER 1985

It has become very difficult
To say the prayer you taught us, Lord.
We suffer at the hands of others so much.
Are we to be the object
Of the Father's Displeasure as well?
For he will not forgive us
Unless we forgive them.
... I have to think this over...
They are forcing me out of my Father's house,
For in this house
There can only be peace and forgiveness.
Stand in our midst, Lord,
And say: PEACE IS WITH YOU.
And may that peace
Re-echo from heart to heart.

Photo: A. Polec.

EASTER 1986

Lord, things are getting worse.
After a while
We shall be unable
To say the prayer you taught us.
We are forgetting how to forgive.
As a consequence the tomb you left empty
Is getting full
Of...corpses.
Stand in our midst
And say: PEACE BE WITH YOU.
For no one but you
Can pronounce it correctly now.

CHRISTMAS 1986

We lift our eyes and hands to heaven.
We are not praying for heaven, Lord.
We pray for food,
For peace, justice and equality,
For love and solidarity
Among men, here on earth.
But now you have confused us, Lord.
It is hard to find you.
For you have come among us,
And imprinted your likeness,
On every human face.
But... why do these faces still reflect
Only conflict, hatred and selfishness?
Is it that, because God became human,
Human beings have decided to step down
And become stones?
Restore us, Lord, to our humanity.

Photo: A. Polec.

16

EASTER 1987

Lord,
If you hear me weeping today,
Do not listen!
For,
If it is strength that I need,
You are my strength.
If it is wisdom,
You have the words of eternal life.
If it is love,
You loved me and died for me.
If it is food,
You have commanded my brothers
To share their food with me.
If it is courage,
You told me to have faith,
And not to fear,
Because You are with me always.
My one problem is that
I continue to weep
And this blurs my vision.
Sometimes I mistake you
For a gardener, or even a ghost.
Forgive me, Lord.

CHRISTMAS 1987

Now, with shaken faith
And fading hope,
We welcome You,
O Prince of Peace,
Into our midst
Though no midst exists for us.
Our greed and inhumanity
Have turned it into cracks.
But you can fit in just the same.
Then, speak the word of peace
And brotherly togetherness,

And we shall be healed,
We count on that word, Lord.

CHRISTMAS 1988

Lord, save us
From this collective amnesia.
We have forgotten
That we were created in God's image;
That in You we are all God's children,
And so, brothers and sisters,
All we need is love and care;
And to be accepted as brothers and sisters,
Just as we are,
We need so little, Lord!
Teach us that we cannot create
Brotherhood out of war.
Give us the good will
To deserve your peace.
Convince at least the Christians
Who welcome you as a Brother,
Not to limit you and your love to
  Bethlehem.
For your heart
Encompasses the whole universe.

EASTER 1989

Risen Lord!
The Doors we closed
To keep out intruders,
To defend our interests,
Have closed us in.
We are now prisoners of our own making.
It is not the closed doors.
It is what we failed to send out
When we closed the doors
That is the only problem.
All breathing space is taken up by
Hatred and revenge,

Cruelty and insensitivity
To human suffering;
Greed and corruption,
Falsehood and dishonesty.
And we are in the firm grip
Of fear, helplessness and despair.
WE ARE SUFFOCATING, LORD!
WE ARE SUFFOCATING, LORD!
Come, stand in our midst.
You are our only hope.

CHRISTMAS 1989

Your birth, Lord, is the Father's hymn
To the glory of every man and woman,
In You each one of them
Is the Father's precious gift to the others.
I think, this Christmas,
Of the poor, the sick, the suffering,
The sinner – despised and shunned,
Of oppressors and persecutors,
And of all men and women of good will.
Without them, we would never become
Compassionate, loving and caring,
Merciful and forgiving,
Patient, forbearing and persevering,
Zealous and thirsting for peace and justice

And committed to your plan
Of building a new world
In which each and every man and woman
Will become a living image of God,
Perfect as the Heavenly Father is.
Help us to value one another
As God has valued us
Just as we are, human beings.

EASTER 1990

It is not the tomb,
Nor the guards
That worry us, Lord;
It is death;
It is the paralysis.
No pain...just dead!
No progress...only decay!
And decay is progressive, Lord.
That is sin.
And injustice, oppression,
Fear, corruption...
And stagnant faith and holiness,
One finds only in tombs!
But the news has spread,
You are Risen,
You, the Resurrection and the Life

Ashes to ashes: Ash Wednesday, Khartoum Cathedral. Photo: A. Polec

For all who believe in you
Even if they be dead.
Others can remove the stone,
But it is me who must come out
In obedience to your command.
GIVE THE ORDER, LORD!
GIVE IT NOW!
Before we disintegrate
Into nothingness!

CHRISTMAS 1990

Your birth, Lord, reminds me
Of the many babies born today
In the desert under the burning sun,
Wrapped in sackcloth and straw,
Victims of human rejection and cruelty.
For them I pray:
May no one ever show them
Where they were born
Except to inspire them
With that love and care
They were denied
And the compassion
Withheld from them.
May they grow to know
That the Son of God
Has shared in and blessed
Their poverty, helplessness
And rejection.
May they learn from you
To bring joy and salvation
To their brothers and sisters
Out of their poverty.

EASTER 1991 (1)

Alleluia
Lord and Saviour,
Strength of the weak,

Hope of the hopeless,
Joy of the sorrowful,
Light in the dark,
Love in the midst of hate,
RISEN FROM THE DEAD,
NEVER TO DIE AGAIN.
No foundation ever so firm.
We see you
We feel your loving presence.
All is life now.
No heads hang in sadness,
No knees knock in fear.
With us is God's glory.
Thank you
For the gift of faith.

EASTER 1991 (2)

Darkness is overwhelming us, Lord.
Everything around us is dark,
Threatening and frightful.
We think now only in terms
Of how things should have been
Or how we hope they will be.
The present is slipping past,
Meaningless and grim.
No matter how deep the darkness,
Your "It is I!" suffices
To give us a sense of direction;
To assure us of a presence;
To fill us with joy and hope.
You did it for the Apostles.
Do it for us now.
It is the sign of your care.

CHRISTMAS 1991

This Christmas,
We pray you, Lord,
For peace – peace for this country,

Many have paid for it
With their blood and tears,
In humiliation and abject misery.
It is enough, Lord!
But others pay
With their blood, their money
And perhaps, their malice
So that there may be no peace.
Do not count it against them.
To pay for
The suffering and the damage
They have caused,
You would have to destroy them.
But you came that all may live.
You are all mercy and forgiveness and love.
May the peace you promised
To people of good will
Flow from them
In torrents of forgiveness and love,
Engulfing and transforming
Also the people of bad will.
May we realise that
Forgiveness, love and solidarity
Are more powerful
Than the force of arms and human malice.
Because they are YOU.

EASTER 1992

Neither hunger nor poverty,
Neither harassment nor injustice
Will silence them, Lord.
They will sing "Alleluia"
For everyone to hear.
I offer you these "Alleluias",
I offer you this joy,
I offer you this faith.
I offer you this witness.
Thank you for this gift.

Without You these young people
Would have been crushed a long time ago.
But now in your strength,
They can praise You.
Are they singing the present or the future.?

CHRISTMAS 1992

The Son of God born of the Virgin,
Is the perfect image
Of the invisible God.
That is disturbing news, Lord.
For there are other images of You,
So disfigured
By hate, corruption,
By suffering, fear and despair.
By sin and so many other evils;
My brothers, sisters and I,
We would like to think and believe
That whoever images You
Should be beautiful and perfect.
But how would we know
That you are there
Where we are most disfigured?
That You, our God,
Are there where we least expect you?
That you are asking us
Not to imagine the God we do not see
But the God who knows disfigurement,
The God who promises and effects
Salvation and wholeness
But from deep within
Not from the glory of heaven,
The brokenness and disfigurement
To which He has united Himself?
Glory to You,
Our God, disfigured
In so many of my brothers and sisters.
And in me!

Glory to your only Son,
Who became like us in all things
Except sin,
Who has given us
The joy to wonder:
GOD IS WITH US!

EASTER 1993

Lord,
The guards, the stone, the seal.
They could not keep you in the grave
But they have now found
Their way to the doors of our hearts
And into your Church.
It was not your wish that
The faith, hope and love,
Kindness, generosity and goodness,
The truth, wisdom and knowledge,
The courage and holiness,
The unity, peace and life
And to top them all;

*Michelle, in Khartoum's Jaborona
displacement camp, with her children,
William and Mary.*

Your Holy Spirit, –
Your resurrection gifts to us –
Should remain dormant,
Imprisoned in our hearts
Or the Church.
Make them come to life
That unbeatable all-pervading life;
Roll back the stone doors,
The doors of fear,
Fear of difficulties and problems.
– the doors of relying on our own strength;
– the doors of human respect.
And what we call our common sense.
– the doors of our sinfulness
and human frailty
– the doors of mediocrity and laziness.
We pray this Easter for Faith, Lord;
Not for faith in your rising to life
But for faith
In your raising us to life with you.
The Good News
Of your resurrection from the dead
Will never spread to the whole world
Without that of our new life in you.
We pray for new vitality
For your Church,
For each one of us.
Call us out of the tomb,
And help us to unbind one another.

CHRISTMAS 1993

I keep wondering, Lord,
Why you, our mighty God,
Were born small,
I believe it was
To set us a pattern: we have to grow.
Babies must grow into adults,
Adults may never grow into babies.

We pray you today
To forgive us for our tendency
Of returning to our cribs
Our origins, our tribes,
When we were born into a wide world,
Born into eternity, born into You.
Forgive us for remaining small
In holiness, in love, in service;
For limiting the world to our friends,
To our pleasures, to our problems.
May we accept from you
This wide world,
So full of Brothers and Sisters,
Of graces and opportunities,
And of the chances to begin again;
This wide world so full of YOU
And of your loving and saving presence.

EASTER 1994 (1)

They saw you die on the cross, and some
   said:
A man, who has died that way, will never
   rise again.
And they carried the day,
With Thomas and those two of Emmaus.
Many of us believe, Lord, that everything is
possible
Except with God.
That is why power, wealth, pleasure,
   prestige,
Are becoming the new gospels of salvation.
So, fear, insecurity, oppression,
Unhappiness, untruth and sin
Have abounded proportionately.
We often write you and your teaching off
As out of touch with reality
As hopeless, and of little help
When troubles are real.

Yet we know
Because you have said it:
If you believe
You will see the glory of God.
Then mountains will move,
Storms calm down, sins be forgiven,
Enemies reconciled, fears dispelled,
Courage restored.
Give to us the grace, Lord,
To live in this troubled world
With faith in You
With whom nothing is impossible.

EASTER 1994 (2)

Lord, today is your question day.
Ask us: "Why are you afraid?"
"What were you discussing on the way?"
We have got used to excluding you, Lord,
From our projects and discussions.
You, the real You, are simply not there:
In our prayers, our work,
Our joys and sorrows
Even if they are
"Through Christ, Our Lord."
For some reason, we prefer
The crucified Lord.
Yet the Lord you want us to remember
Is the Lord, who is risen and alive,
The Lord who has overcome the world;
The Lord of hope;
The Lord who is present to the crucified
To lead from death to life.
That is the Lord who says:
"I am here with you. Why are you afraid?
Do not discuss my death
Or yours with me,
I am risen and so are you."

EASTER 1994 (3)

Lord, I like that part of the gospel:
Those two disciples did not recognise you.
That is when You experienced
What no human being has ever
 experienced:
Hearing people discussing your death and
 burial,
And signing you off as a hopeless case.
And they were so discouraged!
We continue to discourage one another
In your very presence, Lord;
To treat you as a stranger,
To our problems and fears,
So we exaggerate them
And console ourselves
That we are sharing your cross.
You did well to die on a cross:
There is a place for only one person
And you have taken it.
Risen and alive,
You appear unannounced
Wherever there is fear,
Doubt, despair, suffering, and death,
And what peace, joy and courage
You leave behind – when you disappear!
Lord, keep up those mysterious appearances
When we need you most

And may that "most" be always.
And be patient with us, Lord,
When we feel and speak more
Of your death and ours,
Of your pains and ours
Of our sins and failures
Instead of the life and the victory
You have won for us all.

CHRISTMAS 1994

Lord, rumours! Hearsay! Rumours!
Received and handed on.
That is how we often treat
You and your gospel.
A real contagious disease, Lord.
And with substantial payoffs:
We seem holier
And experts in divine matters.
But we are often only echoes,
Hard shiny reflectors of realities
We have not assimilated
Or experienced first hand.
The Shepherds heard of you,
Saw you and then spoke
Of what they heard and saw.
Word of God, you became flesh
Help us to believe that
You are among us.

Suffering in Sudan. Photo: A. Polec

You are not a Saviour
By remote control
But by direct personal involvement.
May the sacraments we celebrate,
Your word we hear and proclaim,
Our life together,
Become real encounters with you.
Be real to us, Lord.
Turn us from hard reflecting walls,
Into sponges saturated
With your presence and word.
May our personal experience of you
Make us true hearers of the Good News:
God is with us.

EASTER 1995

PEACE BE WITH YOU

Lord, you said: "Peace be with you,"
To those unreliable, unfaithful,
Cowardly men who deserted you,
And their fear disappeared:
The fear of the Jews, and fear of you;
And so passed also
The shame and remorse,
The self-pity and hopelessness.
May your merciful and loving eyes
Locate us also
Where we cower with fear, shame,
Sense of lost dignity,
In our effort to avoid
Accusing and pricking fingers;
And where we ourselves
Have forced others to cower.
Say: "Peace" Lord,
Renew our trust in your faithfulness,
Reconciliation and love
And help us to share it with others.
Search for us especially when we sin,

And may our cry for mercy
Always attract your merciful
Forgiving and loving response:
"Peace be with you."

CHRISTMAS 1995

Your birth, Lord
Was news of great joy
For the whole people.
We heard it, Lord.
But we are tight lipped
And tight fisted.
Instead of being channels
Of your joy and peace,
We are often dams
Of fear and greed,
Blocking their flows
The wrong direction.
Break through the dams, Lord.
Let your love and joy flow.
So many are waiting.
Your loving heart
Cannot bear
All the unhappiness,
The despair and fear,
Of our own making,
That fill our world.
Grant your Christian people
The grace to know You,
To appreciate and love
Your saving presence.
May that presence
Draw us together,
Sharing the best we have,
Measuring up to the generosity
Of the love of the Father
Who so loved us
As to send His Only Son.

EASTER 1996

You let the chief priests
Get away with it, Lord.
They bribed the guards! Imagine!
They said You were an impostor.
They said your disciples stole your corpse
And the people believed them.
You did not go to prove to them
That you were risen.
You showed yourself
To your disciples instead.
They needed your presence most.
And here we are, Lord,
Two thousand years
In which saints and martyrs,
And a large army of confessors
Have told us: Christ is alive!
We are often driven to unbelief.
Sin, suffering, and despair shout,
"Where is your God?
If you are sons of God,
Let him deliver you."
We will not ask for deliverance, Lord.
Your presence is deliverance itself.
You said: "I am with you always!"
We believe you, Lord.

CHRISTMAS 1996

Thank you, Lord Jesus
You came into our world
Without money and
Possessions,
Home or company,
Weak and silent.
No sign of eternity
Though from eternity you are.
Yet you were you:
The Saviour, Emmanuel,

God who loves
To be with human beings
Where sin and poverty,
Ignorance, weakness and fear,
Impose an unbearable
Suffocating, paralysing
And enslaving loneliness.
You invite us
To break open the cage
Of sin
To discover your love
Of poverty
To discover your loving care
Of ignorance
To discover your truth
Of weakness
To discover your power
Of fear
To receive your assurance
That you are Emmanuel,
God who saves,
God with us.

EASTER 1997

Full stops, Lord.
They are everywhere.
Human beings like them,
Because they are so easy to write.
But we overuse them, Lord.
Like: I. Want. To. Pray.
Who can want
To pray that way, Lord?
It is so exhausting
Not only the stops
But also those capital letters!
Many cannot write them well.
I thank you, Lord,
You are the Remover of Full Stops

Even for those
Who have run out of ideas
Run out of energy, run out of courage,
Those who think the end has come,
That nothing good
Will ever come their way;
Full stops are dangerous, Lord,
Where the writing is sin,
Discouragement,
Fear, hatred, anger, disappointment.
You, the Remover of Full Stops,
Teach us to know that
No matter what we write,
They are parts
Of an on-going process,
Just incomplete sentences.
Help us to believe that
No sentence in our lives
Is ever complete without You.
When you come last,
We know that what came before
Somehow referred to you;
We know you can begin again
With the correct capital letters.
When we come last, we die.
We will always be last
Unless you teach us
To write your name, a name that says:
You can always begin again
Even if they lay
A huge stone on your tomb.

CHRISTMAS 1997

It is our Family Feast!
Your countrymen challenged you,
Lord
They said you were from Nazareth,
The son of Joseph, a carpenter,

You had no right
To claim you were the Son of God.
Yet you left us this heritage
We too are to call God, Father.
Even from within us
Our sinfulness, our ugliness,
Our limitations, our fears,
Our poverty, our weakness
All band together to say:
"You cannot be children of God".
As if being children of God
Made God less God.
As if God would take us seriously
And become truly our Father
Turning us into small gods?
We prefer to call Him almighty,
Eternal, all-knowing, All-holy God,
In order not to get involved:
For the might, the eternity,
The knowledge and holiness
Are HIS not ours.
But when you told us
God is Love and Father
We have no way of escape.
We know He must love someone,
And you told us:
"That someone is you"!
May all of us
Who come to pay you homage
Be caught up
In the infinite love
That binds you, the Father,
And the Holy Spirit.

EASTER 1998

You foretold it, Lord.
"Strike the shepherd,
The sheep will be scattered."

There was too much sadness,
Too much fear and frustration
Each wanted to nurture his own,
To get out of it his own way.
Then you stepped in.
"Why are you weeping?"
"Why are you alarmed?"
We are surprised, Lord,
That you ask?
And – "How foolish you are
And slow to believe..."
And that is true, Lord.
But it is your breathtaking:
"IT IS I" that reverses everything.
Your words, Lord,
Your promises, your sacraments,
Your church, our very lives
Mean nothing at all
Unless you open our eyes
To recognise you in them all.
Do not count on what we call
Our profession of faith.
See rather, our fears and sorrows.
They paralyse us
Not because of their power,
But because of our foolishness
And slowness to believe...
That: "Christ our Hope is Risen".

You, that Good Shepherd
Who can no longer be stricken,
Now lead us, united, strong
And protected from all dangers
In your victory procession
Into eternal joy and peace.

CHRISTMAS 1998

Great is your birth, Lord
With a message of joy so deep,
A message of hope so high
A message of love so wonderful,
A message of salvation so sure;
The message of a Father
Who loves, and Himself is love,
Who shows mercy,
And Himself is mercy,
Your Father and ours
Who call ourselves human beings
But for you great is small
And small is great!
Human beings have passed you by
These 2,000 years,
And have never really discovered
Love or mercy, joy or hope,
Or the salvation they so desire
Or even a Father
That gathers them together
Into one family,
And loved them
Before they came into being,
And loves them now
In order to love them
Into eternity;
We may not understand this love.
But do not allow us
To ignore or reject it.

Photo: A. Polec.

EASTER 1999

JESUS LIVES! ALLELUIA!

With your death, Lord,
Everything died:
Joy, hope, love, courage.
Even your words and promises
Lost their power and attraction.
Everything becomes frightening.
Threatening and dangerous.
Your disciples
Wouldn't believe
That you were risen
That you were alive...
When you hear us say:
"Jesus is alive,"
We may be shouting out
Our fears and frustrations.
We may be trying
To reassure ourselves.
It is not enough
For you to be alive
You must be alive to us.
If this does not happen,
You are still dead and buried.
It is too much, Lord,
For us to ask
That you show yourself to us,
Victorious, yes,
But with the scars
Of the nails and the spear,
Clear and shining?
Through them
We shall come to know
And believe
That our festering wounds
Are being transformed
Into glorious scars.

CHRISTMAS 1999

Two thousand years,
And your Name has filled our earth!
I wish to call on that Name now:
Jesus! Jesus! Jesus!
And I know I am calling on my God,
My friend, my Saviour,
My life, my light.
You want us to call you also Brother,
Since you taught us to say,
"Our Father," yours and ours.
I invoke you from the terrible
Heart-rending situation we live in.
The word "brother" is losing its meaning.
The word "father"
Has become part of forgotten history
For most of our young people.
We cling to the word "tribe"
Only to exclude and destroy the others.

We are exhausted with living –
The days of Cain,
The tower of Babel
And the oppression
And attempted extermination
Of the sons of Jacob.

Come to update us, Lord,
To your civilisation of love,
Of justice and peace,
Of grace and mutual forgiveness,
Of solidarity and reconciliation
Of truth and integrity,
Help us to know
That we are in the New Testament;
That the old is gone
And the new is here.

May this Jubilee of your Birth,
Bring you to life in our country

And into the life of each one of us.
It is from the depth of misery
That we cry out to you.
Bring hope into this misery.
Be our Saviour, be our Brother,
Be all in all things.
Thank you, Lord Jesus.

EASTER 2000

Alleluia!
That day you really did move;
You were looking for your disciples
You knew where to get them
And you did find them:
Full of fear, full of doubts
Full of worries, full of self-pity
Full of remorse.
You patiently helped them
Get rid of all the accumulated trash.
Then they recognised you.
Then they believed.
There was now room
For your peace, your forgiveness
Your understanding, your power,
Your friendship.

Lord, it is so difficult
To believe good news –
And I say that I believe.
Yet what I really believe in
Are my sins, my weakness
My poverty, my fears,
My self-worth, my ignorance...
Where has my faith in you gone?
The faith and trust in you
As the Saviour, our Saviour,
Who cares for us,
Who loves us,
Who heals us,
Who saves us,
Who understands us, who forgives us,
The all-wise and powerful,
And ever present,
When we need you.
Help me stop
Transferring Good Friday
To Easter Sunday,
And worse still
Turning all my days
Into Good Fridays.
I keep looking for you

The Cardinal presides at a Mass for the great saint, Daniel Comboni, the 19th Century African missionary, (pictured behind).

In the empty tomb.
Tell me: You are Risen, alive
And right here with me.
Help me to believe
For my own sake.

CHRISTMAS 2000

"God so loved...!"
Those are your words, Lord.
We repeat them now,
In order not to forget.
For it is unbelievable,
Not that You love us
But that we can be loved.
It is the story of love as old
As our age in your eternity.
Yet it is ever new –
A love so creative
So all embracing!
The poor, the down trodden,
The outcast, the sinner,
And even the rebel –
All those society
Loathes and shuns –
Find in it
The welcome and dignity
They deserve –
A love without possessiveness,
Never grabbing, or conditioning,
Just inviting, and enabling,
So spacious and all inclusive,
A refuge and direction
For the unsettled and uprooted,
Unintrusively it flows,
Wherever it is welcome.
There was no room for you
In the inns of Bethlehem.
There is room for you now

In the disordered stables
We call our hearts and lives.
In them may you be born
And received with joy,
Wonder and praise.
May it be our turn
To announce the Good News:
Today a Saviour
Has been born to us:
He is Christ the Lord.

CHRISTMAS 2001

Lord, we have heard of your wonderful
    deeds!
You saved. You forgave. You taught.
You encouraged. You healed. You cared.
Crowds flocked to see, to hear and to
    touch you.
Power came out of you and healed them
    all.
So we acclaim you this year: today
Your name is: "Saviour".
We do not come to praise or adore you.
No need for you to come to earth the
    way you did
to receive our puny adoration and praise.
You came to save.
We come to be saved, Lord,
From our unwillingness to be saved, our
    resistance to salvation.
If you talk of and bring us holiness, love
    and forgiveness,
Truth, life, light and hope.
We desire all this
But we are afraid. They will change us,
    Lord.
It is too much for us.
Save us, Lord, from being too small;

Too calculating and narrow minded;
Save us, Lord, from the falsehood and the
    trap
Of trying to do it all on our own.
We see only the difficulty in what you offer
    us –
And even if there isn't any, we create it.
We feel so satisfied,
When we declare something is difficult
May we accept the good news:
"With God nothing is impossible"
And the good news you repeat every
    Christmas,
The good news of your presence:
"I am with you always!"
May we welcome you, Lord
And come to be saved
Happy Birthday, Jesus!

EASTER 2002

Your presence, Lord.
We all desire it. We invoke it.
This is our faith
For you are Risen
And are actively alive.
We often forget that
You had to suffer and die
In order to enter into your glory.
That is why
We create and look for shortcuts:
To life without death
To glory without pain
To holiness without repentance
To joy without sorrow
To discipleship without the cross.
We continuously pray for deliverance
For mercy, for strength.
We even challenge

Your power, your compassion,
We attempt to remove
Our tomb stones on our own.

But you are risen, Lord –
Risen from death.
Help us to notice
The scars of your wounds,
Witnessing to your presence
Where there are wounds –
To your power
Where there is weakness –
To your grace
That is always sufficient –
To your promise of glory,
That far surpasses all our troubles.
May we share in your suffering,
Become like you in your death
So as to experience
The power of your resurrection.

*Children and their teacher at a school in
Masalma parish, Omdurman, Khartoum, on
the banks of the River Nile.*

CHRISTMAS 2002

Word of God, You became flesh:
One with us, living our lives
In a solidarity and closeness
That not only escapes
But also surpasses
All description and understanding!
How we wish to see your glory!
How we wish that glory
Of the only Son of the Father
To fill our lives and inspire
All we are and do!
How we wish to feel that glory
Reflected on our faces
And on the faces of all we meet.
If only our faces
Were reflective enough!
Yet we have the courage and faith
To appropriate to ourselves
That all-pervading glory,
As in every Eucharistic Celebration:
We exclaim:
"Through Him, with Him,
And in Him!"
In order to perfect our praise
To your Father and our Father,
And so be transformed
Into your likeness:
Ourselves becoming day by day
Truly beloved children of the Father
Through you, with you, and in you.
We thank and praise you
For your Incarnation
And rejoice
In your redeeming presence,
O Emmanuel, God with us.

EASTER 2003

There are situations, Lord.
Most seem irreversible.
And painfully so.
For you, the ones you create,
They are indeed, irreversible –
But different from ours.
They come in terms
Of joy without end,
Of life without end,
Of hope unbreakable,
Of treasures none can steal,
Of horizons beyond sight,
Of things beyond imagination.
The impossible becomes possible.
Dream becomes reality.
The little ones become great,
The sinner holy,
The doubtful certain,
The darkness light.
The truth of it, Lord,
Is that you are there,
You are here.
Make your presence truly,
Blessing in our sour days,
Blessing in our sinfulness,
Blessing in our helplessness,
Blessing in our death,
The Blessing of faith and hope,
The Blessing of eternal life.
While we walk the earth,
You are not yet fully risen
Until your least brothers and sisters
Rise fully with you and in you.
Help us to rid ourselves
Of tomb stones sealed
With our poverty and weakness.
But what are tomb stones

For you who enters
Where doors are locked?
Come uninvited
For you are Lord and Saviour!

CHRISTMAS 2003

Lord Jesus, I welcome you.
Yet I wonder
If you feel truly welcome.
I wonder too:
Is mine a true welcome?
Or, have I turned you
Into a mere beehive
Precious when full of honey
Useless when emptied
Ready to be discarded.
"Emptied" is the word, Lord –
A bad word.
It can mean "impoverished"
Nothing more to give!
Nothing but itself!
But it can also mean bounty:
An unlimited supply,
Always there for the asking.

In you, the two converge:
Poverty and abundance:
Nothing possessing,
Nothing to give but yourself.
In you we find abundance
Of generous love,
Of merciful compassion,
Of hope and salvation,
Of divine presence.
Continuously reaching out,
You extend yourself totally
Into our emptiness,
Filling it with your presence.
Nature abhors a vacuum.
Make us aware of our emptiness
Not a silent emptiness,
But one that calls out:
Come, Lord Jesus,
Keep coming.
There is always room for you.
A seat reserved for you.
Come, Lord Jesus,
Before I fill it
Even with myself!

A displacement camp in Khartoum a few hours after indiscriminate bulldozing by the Sudanese authorities.

II
Pastoral Letters for Christmas and Easter

EASTER MESSAGE 1986

Jesus came and stood among them. "Peace be with you," he said. "If you forgive people's sins, then they are forgiven." (Jn 20:19,23)

I am addressing you – all of you; you who suffer because of the misdeeds of others – you, victims of exploitation, oppression, discrimination and various types of injustices, you, the homeless and the hungry, also, you, who live in homes without joy and peace, perhaps because of an alcoholic, quarrelsome, cruel and irresponsible husband or father, a nagging and troublesome wife or mother, an unfaithful partner, or hard-headed and heartless children. All of you, who trace your sufferings and unhappiness to the malice or negligence of other people, I am addressing YOU ALL.

Jesus is risen. The very Jesus, who was accused falsely, insulted, tortured and crucified, IS RISEN.

I feel that he should have appeared first to Pontius Pilate, Caiaphas and company just to frighten them to death. He should at least have appeared to the guards to rebuke them about their lies regarding his resurrection. He did neither. He appeared to his disciples instead.

He had already said his last word about his murderers: "Forgive them, Father. They don't know what they are doing." (Lk 23:34) On the first day of his risen life, he had another message for them. He told his disciples that: "In his name, the message about repentance and the forgiveness of sins must be preached to all nations, beginning in Jerusalem." (Lk 24:47)

The message about repentance and the forgiveness of sins was to be preached FIRST to those who killed him, beginning in Jerusalem. The new programme of forgiveness was to start from the disciples: "If you forgive people's sins, they are forgiven." Just like that.

The resurrection of Christ and the gift of the Holy Spirit have filled the earth with forgiveness. We are witnesses to these things. At this Easter, we are going to have the courage to proclaim forgiveness and to be the first to forgive. We are going to forgive all "those who trespass against us", just as God has first forgiven us.

I am appealing to you, disciples of Christ in this country,

Photo: A. Polec

to initiate the programme of reconciliation and peace, through the forgiveness of sins, particularly those committed against us.

Your faith in the reality and the cruelty of Christ's passion and death obliges you to follow his example in the forgiveness of enemies. Your sharing in his resurrection, through Baptism, obliges you to proclaim peace, repentance and forgiveness of sins.

Hatred, division, cruelty, violence and revenge have filled our country. Hatred plus hatred adds up to more hatred. Revenge plus revenge adds up to more revenge. May this sort of addition not take part in our hearts.

You know each and everyone who does you wrong, (but) Jesus calls you…to sow love where there is hatred.

The call to forgiveness is not an abstract idea. There are people, living people, who need forgiveness right now. You know people who are indiscriminately bombing innocent and unnamed villagers. You know those who are breeding violence – the kind of violence called injustice, oppression, exploitation and discrimination. You know who are provoking the "holy" war. You know each and every one who does you wrong because we generally keep accurate records of offences.

Jesus calls you to break away from this group to join him. Your task henceforth is to sow love where there is hatred, forgiveness where there are offences and sins, and peace where there is conflict. At Easter, we must force ourselves to join in Jesus' prayer: "Forgive them, Father. They don't know what they are doing." For indeed they don't know.

In the precincts of St. Matthew's Cathedral, Khartoum, seat of the Cardinal.

Christ died and rose from the dead for all men. Through us, he wants his salvation to reach them all, particularly those who need salvation most but are unable to ask for it because they don't know how to. Christ is waiting for us to pronounce the word of pardon so that he may add: "I do not condemn you either. Go, but do not sin again." (Jn 8:11)

Join me in praying that all of us may rise this Easter from the tomb of hatred, division, revenge and violence. We have no appointment with these messengers of death. Our appointment is with…

THE RISEN LORD. And his greeting is: "PEACE BE WITH YOU."

EASTER MESSAGE 1987
"GET OUT OF THAT TOMB"

Dear Brothers and Sisters,

"Christ is risen!" The great stone has been rolled from the mouth of the tomb. The seal of Pilatus has been broken. The armed guards have taken fright and fled. "CHRIST IS RISEN! The tomb is empty! Death will no longer have power over him." The struggle between good and evil, between life and death, will continue. But Christ has now guaranteed for all times that good will overcome evil and that life will overcome death.

Isn't this a strange message for most of you? For you who today mourn the cruel and unjust death of your loved ones? For you who groan under the yoke of injustice and oppression? For you who have fled into hiding "for fear of the Jews"? For you who have lost all hope in the future, and, because of that loss, find no meaning in life? For you who are burdened by sin and unfaithfulness to your Christian vocation in spite of your struggle to free yourselves? NO! THE MESSAGE IS NOT STRANGE. This is a message for you, and especially for you. It has been faithfully handed down to us by the very apostles and disciples who witnessed Christ's crucifixion and who felt as HOPELESS AS YOURSELVES. But a radical change came over them when they saw and recognised the Risen Lord. His presence among them brought JOY, HOPE, STRENGTH, COURAGE, PURPOSE, and DETERMINATION.

Sister Betty, from Wau, Cardinal Zubeir's home town in south Sudan.

The greatest danger confronting us today is that of despair, the loss of hope. Only the Risen Lord can restore hope to those who believe in him. For the Lord who rose from the dead is the same Lord who was crucified, died and was buried. He is the same Lord who on the Cross reached such a depth of helplessness that he cried out: "My God, my God, why have you forsaken me?" (Mt 27:46) No wonder his resurrection brought the disciples such relief. At the beginning of his public life, he approached the disciples where they were and called them: "Follow me". Now at the beginning of his risen life, he met them where they were, in their fear and despair, and called them: "Follow me". But now they know that this man, Jesus, was not a deceiver. And they followed him. They went out in his company to overcome evil, to give hope and courage to human beings, and to proclaim the good news that people can come out of their graves and live.

Jesus, now risen from the dead, comes to us where we are, in our fear and despair, to complete his first call to us. The first call was: "Take up your cross and follow me." The call now is: "Come out of that tomb and follow me. Break those seals. Roll away that stone. Scatter those guards. Come out and live."

We have accepted to follow Christ through suffering and death. But why is it so difficult to follow him to life? Now he invites us to break out of the tombs that imprison us: the tomb of hatred and division; the tomb of greed and selfishness; the tomb of sin, deliberate and habitual sin; the tomb of lack of faith and trust in God; the tomb of paralysis and helplessness, that prevents us from using the resources for survival and life God has built into our very being. Our experience of these "tombs" reveals that they bring death: death to others and death to ourselves. They bring unhappiness to us and to others. They limit our scope in life to mere self-defence and the struggle for mere survival.

The special message of the Risen Lord as He stands today in our communities is: "There is more life outside these tombs." There is love, given and received, which turns the whole world into a brotherhood in which no one is threatened by another, and no one feels the need to defend himself against others. There is peace and reconciliation that cures the hurts we have received and inflicted. There is the sharing of the resources of life that excludes no one and leaves no one in need. There is the determination and commitment to struggle out of difficulties. This reassures us and convinces us that we have the capability to cope with life.

Jesus Christ, who died and remained three days in the tomb, is risen. He is our guarantee that we also have come out of our tombs, out of anything that paralyses us and prevents us from living the fullness of our lives as human beings created in God's image and likeness. Easter is an invitation for us to pass with Christ from death to life. His words of reassurance are: "I AM ALWAYS WITH YOU." But he will not be with us in the tomb. If he happens to be in the tomb with us, He will break loose, opening for us a way to get out. CHRIST HAS SPOKEN HIS WORD OF VICTORY!

TO ALL OF YOU, MY BROTHERS AND SISTERS, HAPPY EASTER.

The greatest danger confronting us today is that of despair. Only the Risen Lord can restore hope.

CHRISTMAS MESSAGE 1987
GOOD NEWS OF GREAT JOY FOR THE WHOLE PEOPLE

Brothers and Sisters,

Year after year, in times of peace or war, of famine or plenty, joy or sorrow, and of hope or despair, we greet one another at Christmas with: "Happy Christmas!", and we invoke God's blessings and peace upon one another. This custom began on the very night Christ was born. An Angel of the Lord appeared to a group of shepherds and announced to them the good news of great joy - a joy to be shared by the whole people. A little while later, the host of angels sang the praises of God and wished peace to men on earth. This was the first time in human history that one single piece of news became good news of great joy for the whole people.

The Good News was: "Today…a Saviour has been born to you; he is Christ the Lord." (Lk 2:11) It was the proclamation of the truth that God loved us so much that he sent his Son as Saviour of the world, so that we could have life through him; so that, through him, we may gain our freedom, the forgiveness of our sins; so that in him we may become God's adopted children entitled to call God "Abba - Father - My Father."

> The Good News must break out of the darkness of war, division and hatred that overshadow our country.

The news of the Saviour's birth was also the Good News of human togetherness. For in him we become brothers and sisters to one another, children of the one heavenly Father. He is truly "the peace between us". In his person, He has killed all hostility. He replaced hatred with love, revenge with forgiveness, and domination with service, selfishness with generosity, even to the point of giving oneself to and for others. And He himself became the greatest preacher of the Good News and announced that a new era had begun.

Just as the first Christmas marked the beginning of a new era in human history, so each one of us is called to make this Christmas the beginning of a new era in our relationships with God and with one another.

Every "Happy Christmas", besides being a greeting, must become the proclamation of the good news of great joy for the whole people: the good news of union with God; the good news of unity and solidarity among ourselves; the good news of reconciliation and peace, of dialogue and understanding. The Good News must break out of the darkness of war, division and hatred that now overshadows our country. It must replace the language of war with that of peace and brotherhood.

The language of war is unmistakable. It expresses everything in terms of relations of force, of group and class struggles, and of friends and enemies. It creates social barriers. It breeds contempt of others. It creates an atmosphere of hatred and terrorism. The language of war is not good news for the whole people.

The language of war falsifies the message of Christmas. Its frequent use in our society is a clear sign that we desperately need a Saviour. We need a Saviour who will free us from tribal, racial, social and religious hostilities. We need a Saviour who will break the walls of enmity, hatred, falsehood and revenge. That Saviour is already among us. He calls for our co-operation. Let us help him break down the walls of division and hatred.

At this Christmas, I urge you all, brothers and sisters, not to use the greeting "Happy Christmas" merely out of habit. Let it become a true affirmation of your stand for peace, and your determination to work for peace. For a good language means nothing if it is not the expression of what is in our hearts. Such a language is also futile unless it is accompanied by gestures of peace. For it is the practice of peace that leads to peace.

May all the disciples of Christ in this country raise their voices with the angels to proclaim peace to all men of good will. May they become those men and women of good will who promote peace in their families, among their friends and wherever Providence has placed them. The only good news of great joy, a joy to be shared by the whole Sudanese people today, is the Good News of Peace. If we Christians allow ourselves to be carried away by the language of war, where shall we find the courage and the strength to sing: "Glory to God in the highest, and peace on earth to men of good will"?

Starting with this Christmas, every Sunday will be a frightful challenge to our sincerity.

HAPPY CHRISTMAS TO YOU ALL. I have chosen to speak of Peace instead of War. Amen.

A thanksgiving sacrifice will I make: Mass for the Archbishop after his return to Khartoum as Cardinal.

CHRISTMAS MESSAGE 1988

This year also we dare to celebrate Christmas.

We respond to the Angel's announcement of the news of great joy, which shall be for the whole people: "This very day...your Saviour was born - Christ the Lord." (Lk 2:11) This is the child of whom the Angel Gabriel spoke to Mary: "He will be great and will be called the Son of the Most High God." (Lk 1:32) With the birth of this child, God, who had created man in his own image and likeness, now becomes God in the image and likeness of man. And this because "God loved the world so much..." (Jn 3:16) God, who is love, became man so that human beings may in their turn become love and loving. Christ's birth is the beginning of a great re-ordering, the re-ordering of man's relationship with God: God is your loving Father in heaven; and of man's relationship with his fellow men: "You are all brothers." (Mt 23:8)

"Today, your Saviour was born." This is the kind of Saviour the Sudanese people await today - the One who came to be a brother to each one of you, and has in himself made you brothers to one another. Christmas is indeed the feast of universal brotherhood - the feast of God's love, dwelling bodily among men and making them sharers in that love.

How I wish that this message rang throughout the Sudan today and penetrated into the deepest recesses of every heart. Let it ring out clearly and convincingly at least from the hearts, the mouths and the lives of all who believe in Christ. May the message read: "Because of the Word of God made man - a man like us in all things but sin - every man is my brother." MY BROTHER. MY BROTHER.

What a difficult word to say. How difficult it is to be a brother to everybody. How difficult it is to say it to the one who has killed your parents and children; to the one from whom you escaped with your life by a miracle; to the one who has robbed you of your possessions; to the one who has rendered you homeless; to the one who is bent on starving you to death; to the one before whom you are nothing but a dog. Yet it is the word we must say at Christmas. For Christmas is the day on which God himself reaffirms the equal dignity of every human being, the basic principle of human brotherhood and solidarity, the respect and love due to each human being, precisely because he or she is a human being. He did that by becoming himself a human being so that thereafter no one may hate, despise or maltreat another human being without hating, despising or maltreating God.

Our quest for peace can be sensible and serious only if it is based on

> How I wish that this message rang throughout the Sudan today and penetrated into the deepest recesses of every heart.

the principle of brotherhood, that is, on our acknowledging and treating each and every man or woman as our brother or sister. The argument for peace cannot be the unity of the country. It cannot be the improvement of the economy or the prevention of foreign intervention in the country. For all these can be achieved over the corpses of thousands of people. The victorious cry for peace is: "Every man is my brother." – "Every Sudanese is my brother." The cry for war is the denial of brotherhood. The cry for war is the denial of God who created the brotherhood and himself became part of it.

Even human wisdom has reached the point of affirming: "All human beings are born free and equal in dignity and rights. They are endowed with reason and conscience and should act towards one another in a spirit of brotherhood." (U.N. Declaration of Human Rights). And if all of us are peace-makers, Christ's words will be fulfilled in us: "Happy are those who work for peace: God will call them his children." They will be children of the same Father, the Father of our Lord Jesus Christ, and therefore, brothers to one another. Brothers and Sisters, let us live Christmas. This is what I mean as I greet you all.

HAPPY CHRISTMAS.

EASTER MESSAGE 1992

Dear Brothers and Sisters,

With joy we celebrate Christ's resurrection. He has triumphed over death and sin and all related evils, and stands now among us offering us the certainty of our own triumph over death, sin and related evils. Easter is therefore our celebration as well.

You will have realised that the gospel accounts of Christ's resurrection say very little about Christ himself except that He was risen, and went about showing himself to his disciples and strengthening their faith in his resurrection.

We hear more about the disciples, and what they did in the power of the Risen Lord. We hear of the great change that took place in them. They run about to break the news of Christ's resurrection to one another, they are full of joy at the sight of the Lord, they BELIEVE, and later, they bear courageous witness to Christ's resurrection, completely defying threats, imprisonment and death. They experience a complete turn about: from sorrow to joy, doubt to certainty, fear to courage, despair to hope, helplessness to strength, aimlessness to determination and a fixed direction in their lives and activities – and what a great love and attachment to Christ they developed! What a great trust in His power working through them.

To appreciate this change, we have to go back to the events of Good Friday and see the great and massive build-up of evil. It starts from a small group of people and soon spreads into the crowds. It develops fast and with full force, crushing before it all that is good and praiseworthy in human beings. It does away with reason and elementary common sense, with truth and justice, with compassion and mercy. It crushes everyone who upholds these values. Every good gives way before the might of lies, cruelty, hatred and self-interest. Evil crushes Jesus to the point of making him cry out: "My God, my God, why have you abandoned me?" – and those who upheld evil believed that they had won.

Even the disciples believed that evil had won. They hid away in fear. They were desperate: with a present from which there was no escape and a future that was too dark to imagine. They were disillusioned. And I think they began to hate Jesus, whom they could well consider to be the cause of all their problems.

This Easter, we find ourselves in the condition of Jesus and the disciples. Evil, injustice, falsehood, cruelty and their derivatives loom so powerfully – they seem unbeatable. We know what sadness, discouragement, fear, despair and helplessness are. We celebrate Easter in the midst of it all. We proclaim: Jesus is risen, Jesus is alive. The proclamation, however, remains incomplete if it does not include: "...And we are risen with him. We are part of his triumph over death and sin."

Suffering will continue. Every type of evil will continue. We however live in the certainty that every evil contains in itself the seeds of its own destruction. Every excess it indulges in quickens its own destruction and hastens the triumph of good. The victims of evil are already winning through their very sufferings: sowing the seeds of forgiveness, patience, and above all, trust in God. And this God who raised Jesus from the dead will exercise the same power in favour of those who put their trust in Him.

The disciples took to proclaiming Jesus as the only Saviour and Lord. Nothing could stop them from it. They knew that their silence would mean the unchallenged continuation of evil and sin. So even under torture they continued to proclaim that Jesus is Lord. This is why neither threats, nor harassment, nor imprisonment should stop or frighten us into silence or fear. In the power of Jesus, we must stand up for truth, for justice, for love, for human dignity and rights. The consequences of silence will be: falsehood, injustice, hatred, cruelty –

and the suppression of other human beings will continue. That means more suffering, more unhappiness, more disorder among men. It is the prolongation of Good Friday.

May this Easter open our eyes to see Jesus and to recognise him present with us in all our difficulties and sufferings, and to see him leading us into freedom and joy. May our troubles and even death become seeds of life being sown now for a great harvest, which the Lord guarantees will come about. For it is not by our strength that we can bring about the transformation but by God's power. No one can defeat God. Nothing is impossible with God.

Do you believe this? Then take courage. Hold your head high. The Risen Lord is with you.

Happy Easter!

Threats, harassment, imprisonment should not stop or frighten us into silence or fear.

CHRISTMAS MESSAGE 1996

A Reason to thank God
That all our prayers have not been answered

Someone told me this story.

Two women were fighting. Neither of them could get the better of the other. One of them turned to prayer: "Mother Mary, help me to knock her down." The other woman promptly thought of a counter prayer: "Mother Mary, do not listen to her, rather help me to knock her down." The storyteller did not tell me how the fight ended. I only think that Mother Mary was truly embarrassed and perplexed.

Each one wants to have God all for himself or herself. So we "create" as many gods as are our interests and needs. Christians have their "Christian God", and Muslims their "Muslim God"; Northerners their "Northern God" and "Southerners their "Southern God". And what terrible Gods! How would the one God, who is Father of all, hear the prayer of one who seeks help to kill or harm another? How would he accept the praise and thanks of one who rejoices in God's name over the defeat or misfortune of a brother or sister? Yet that is the way we pray at least some of the time. We don't realise that in this way we contradict our faith in one and only one God, the Creator of all and the Father of all. And the way we pray makes us the kind of persons we are. We fashion our gods "to our own likeness": selfish, greedy, cruel, proud, deceitful, sectarian, discriminating...and also foolish. And we become more selfish, greedy, cruel... It is usually "a god" who excludes the poor, the humble, and powerless, and excludes poverty, humility and what else we imagine to be undesirable. For us it is "a god" who should

Andrew, aged five, sits in the chapel of a displacement in Wau, south Sudan.

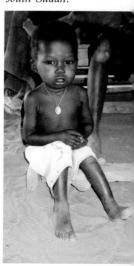

reserve every good thing for us. If he distributes anything to us all, then ours should be better.

Christmas, the feast of God who became a human being and was born of the Virgin Mary, is the beginning of a new way of knowing and "seeing" God. Human beings have fashioned enough of their own gods: national gods, tribal gods, family gods... who celebrate with them their national and family feasts, hate those they hate, fight their tribal and personal wars...who can be sold and bribed. And of course these gods could be as cruel or gentle, honest or dishonest, powerful or weak as those who made them.

Christmas comes with a message of a Saviour, come to dwell amongst us and with us, Jesus, the one Saviour of the human race, yesterday, today and forever. He is the Saviour who "has made salvation possible for all men," at whose birth the angels announced the "joy, which shall be for the whole people".

He came to save the poor and the rich, the sinners and the upright, the wise and the foolish...irrespective of their colour, sex, or tribe. A Saviour is for those who need salvation. But if God left it entirely to us, many of us would never be saved, because we do not know our needs. We so often confuse opportunities with needs. For many of our needs are really opportunities, opportunities in which God dwells, in which God's presence is felt, and which God has taken upon himself. They are opportunities for us to meet God and to co-operate with him in his work of salvation.

This Saviour was born in Bethlehem, in a tiny insignificant village. The Saviour was born poor, homeless, helpless, unknown and completely dependent on others for his very survival. Like every new-born child, he could not speak. If he was not born that way, then he was not a real human child. But this child was also God, the only begotten Son of God. We should today renew, feel and express our faith in Jesus Christ "Emmanuel", that is in "God (who) - is - with - us". This presence makes all of us great. It makes all that discourages us encouraging; all that saddens us joy giving. It makes all that drives us to despair sources of hope. Weakness becomes strength. Sin is not merely forgiven but transformed into uprightness. Fear is dispersed and replaced with courage, faith and hope. Human beings become children of God. There is no longer someone to knock down because we would be knocking God down too. From when God has come to us, we can only go upwards.

We run from poverty, dependence, hardship, situations of need and humiliation... God embraces them, revives them and exalts them. Our problem is that these very conditions make us angry, envious, greedy...

The presence (Emmanuel) makes all of us great...it makes all that drives us to despair sources of hope.

To overcome them we steal, rob, and grab. We grumble and complain. We fight and destroy one another. We even lose faith and trust in God.

From now on, our faith should be able to tell us: our poverty is God's poverty, and so are our humiliation, our helplessness, our despair, our homelessness...not only that but also: God's wealth has become ours, and so also have his power, his patience, his goodness, mercy and compassion, his holiness...And above all, that God is one of us. And the Son of God adds one more thing: God loves us all.

God, who sent his only Son to save humankind, wants to take back his only Son together with the whole human race he was sent to save. The Son has descended to the lowest in order to lift all up. The best way to carry several pieces of bamboo is to bind them together and to lift the bundle from the bottom. May the faith that drives us to implore from God the salvation for which he sent his Son, lead us to implore it for all our brothers and sisters. From now on, no one can implore God for help or protection except through and with Emmanuel, "God with us". "Through Him, with Him and in Him", there is only one prayer: "Our Father", who is to be glorified in the highest heaven, and who in his turn imparts "peace on earth" to all who call him Father, the Father of our Lord Jesus Christ and Our Father, the Father of the whole human race and of all who are aware of what Fatherhood means, namely: that we are all brothers and sisters in the great family in which Jesus Christ is the first born.

I wish you all a Happy Christmas.

We can all be happy, without wishing to knock anyone down or asking God to do it on our behalf.

We run from poverty, dependence, hardship and humiliation. God revives and exalts...

Khartoum priests Frs. Todo (left) and Guido

CHRISTMAS MESSAGE 1998

"God so loved the world..."

And so we celebrate Christmas.

We want to hear again and feel deep in our beings the Good News that God loved us so much that he sent us his only Son. (Cf. Jn 3:16)

God has never been lacking in his love for the human race. For his love is everlasting and ever faithful. In fact, "God is love". (1 Jn 4:8)

God created the human being with great care and tenderness. Scripture tells us that man and woman came into the world by a very direct and personal decision and action of God: "Then God said: 'Let us make man in our image, in the likeness of ourselves...'"; and accordingly, "male and female he created them". (Cf. Gen 1:24-7) Then, "God shaped man from the soil of the ground and blew the breath of life into his nostrils and man became a living being." (Gen 2:7) No other creature was created with the same attention and care.

But images can be disfigured. Likewise, the breath of life can be breathed out.

Comboni missionary, Fr. Angelo, with refugee children in the town of Kosti, 150 miles south of Khartoum.
Photo: A. Polec

46

However, God in his wisdom, love and mercy, and from all eternity, willed to restore his image in us, and blow into us a new breath of life that cannot be breathed out. Yes, he sent us his only Son in accordance with his plan to mark us out beforehand to be his adopted children through Jesus Christ. (Cf. Eph 1:5) He sent the Spirit of his Son, the spirit of adoption, into our hearts to enable us to cry out: "Abba! Father!" - and to join with our spirit to bear witness that we are children of God. (Cf. Rom 8:15-16)

This is what Christmas is: the Son of God becomes a human being, and human beings become children of God.

Jesus Christ, who is the perfect image of the unseen God, enters fully into our human condition in everything except sin. He took upon himself our weakness, misery, helplessness, poverty and dependence. And, born of a woman, as every one of us was, he is of one blood with us, and is not ashamed to call us his brothers and sisters. (Cf. Hb 2:11)

We may never understand this love.

Because he is the Son of God, he brings into our human condition the infinite love, mercy and care of the Father - his Father and our Father, his God and our God - that God who is love and mercy. For he can never be separated from the love of the Father.

Because of the presence of God's Son in our minds, we no longer need to struggle for God's love and mercy. For God's love and mercy are always present to those who, forgetting themselves, their misery and sin, dare to cry out, even with tears: "Abba! Father!"

We may and will suffer hardships, or distress, or persecution, or lack of food and clothing, or threats or violence. One thing is however, always certain. "...We came through all these things triumphantly victorious, by the power of him who loved us." (Rom 8:37)

Christmas invites and urges us to recognise for ourselves and to put our faith in the love that God has for us, the love he revealed to us when he sent his only Son to be our brother and to live among us. Clouds may at times be very dark, but the sun continues to shine undiminished above us. So it is with God's all-powerful, ever-present, and ever-faithful love that radiates from his only Son, the Emmanuel, who is God with us.

We may never fully understand this love.

May Christmas help us

Never to ignore or reject it.

GOD LOVES YOU!

CHRISTMAS MESSAGE 1999

Brothers and Sisters,

"The mercy of God the Father, the love of the Word Incarnate, and the fellowship of the Holy Spirit be with you all."

"When the right time finally came, God sent his own Son. He came as the son of a human mother...so that we might become God's sons. To show that you are his sons, God sent the Spirit of his Son into our hearts, the Spirit who cries out: 'Father, my Father.'" (Gal 4:4-6)

At Christmas, we hear the Good News: "The Word became a human being and full of grace and truth, lived among us." (Jn 1:14) It is the news about Emmanuel, "God is with us." This year, the news adds a truly new dimension: God has been with us in this form for 2,000 years. We in the Sudan have experienced this presence for 100 years. We have to listen to the Angel's song: "Glory to God in the highest heaven, and peace on earth to those with whom he is pleased." This year that song must be sung louder. For it is not the first announcement. It is the announcement of 2,000 years of God's presence in Jesus Christ. It is the announcement of 2,000 years of his presence in the Church and in some way in each one of us, because we are members of this Church.

Jaborona displacement camp outside Khartoum. Assistant priest Fr. John said all night vigils were held in the church to prevent it from demolition by Government security services.

Our own 100 years of Christ's visible presence in this country ought to "force" each one of us to raise a resounding hymn of praise and thanksgiving to God. We thank and praise him for the special way in which he has led us to "reproduce" the presence of Christ in this country. I do not refer only to the Church in the Sudan, but to each one of you who in your diversity have given to this Church an identity. You have given Christ a face by which he can be recognised.

We witnessed not only to his glory and power. We witnessed also to him as a sign of contradiction and became in him signs of contradiction ourselves. We have shown ourselves as God's servants and fellow servants, like St Paul, with Jesus "by patiently enduring troubles, hardships and difficulties. We have been beaten, imprisoned or mobbed; we have been overworked, and have gone without sleep or food. By our purity, knowledge, patience and kindness, we have shown ourselves to be God's servants - by the Holy Spirit, by our true love, by our message of truth, and by the power of God ...We are honoured and disgraced; we are insulted and praised. We are treated as liars, yet we speak the truth; we are treated as if we are unknown, yet we are known by all; as though we were dead, but as you see, we live on. Although punished, we are not killed; although saddened, we are always glad; we seem poor, but we make many people rich; we seem to have nothing, yet we really possess everything." (2 Cor 6:4–10) This is the contradiction of the Son of God who: "became a human being and lived among us".

In the midst of our joy, thanksgiving and praise, we need to allow the second part of the Angels' song to resound in our country. Peace on earth was announced when the Son of God was born into poverty and human weakness. By his birth he has empowered the poor and the weak to be peacemakers. We cannot identify with Christ's poor unless we truly become peacemakers. Our tools for peace are our endurance, our patience, our power to forgive, our solidarity with one another, our unity, and our trust in God's power. For the Son of God became a human being so that human beings might become children of God.

Christmas is our birthday as children of God. May Christians recognise their dignity and new identity. May they take it as seriously as Christ took his humanity. May that seriousness help each of us to break through the walls of division that have so terribly wrecked our communities and nation.

This Christmas of the Great Jubilee ought to become a turning point in our history. We have to add a new chapter to our presence in the Sudan. In that chapter, we will no longer identify ourselves as Ndogo, Zande, Nuer, Dinka, Lotuho ... with each one claiming for himself the right to jump at the other's throats ... but simply as "Children of God!" - that means, Brothers and Sisters. Then the Angels will sing: "Glory to God in the highest heaven, and peace on earth to those with whom he is pleased." That song will be heard only when the children of God are born. Then there will be news of great joy for the whole people!

I wish you all a truly Happy Christmas.
May the Jubilee help all of us
To walk together in the way of peace.
May it be a year of life, not of death.
The Prince of Life is now "God with us!"

Our tools for peace are endurance, patience, our power to forgive, our solidarity with one another and our trust in God's power.

49

EASTER MESSAGE 2001

To the Christian Young People – Archdiocese of Khartoum

Dear Young (and not so Young) People, Brothers and Sisters,

Jesus met the women who had gone to anoint his body and told them: "Do not be afraid. Go and tell my brothers to go to Galilee and there they will see me." (Mt 28:10). After the breakfast at the lakeside, He said to Peter: "Follow me." Jesus had said something similar to Peter and his companion fishermen before: "Come after me and I will make you fishers of men." (Mt 4:19). He called each of the other disciples in the same way: "Follow me."

I now invite you to look at the crosses I gave you on 1st January 2001 at the end of the Youth Congress. They bear the words: "Follow me!" – You know that those are Jesus' words. But he is not on that cross. If he is still on the cross, he is either dying or already dead. Dead men don't talk. Jesus who calls you to follow him is the Jesus who was on the cross, who died and was buried but who is now risen from the dead and alive. Jesus wants you to follow him into victory, new life and freedom.

The message of Easter is that we have to follow Jesus who is alive. "Why do you seek the living among the dead?" (Lk 21-5) He cannot be among the dead because he is the resurrection and the life. (Cf. Jn 11:25) In fact, he came "that they might have life and have it more abundantly." (Cf. Jn 10:10) What Jesus is saying is: "Follow me into life. Follow me into freedom – the true freedom of the children of God. Join me in my victory." The empty cross is the sign of all this.

This is the first Easter of the Third Millennium, which I asked you to claim as your millennium. In fact, this millennium is being founded on you, with you and by you. Jesus tells you to follow him. You follow someone who is ahead of you: "Follow me" is the language of the present – where he is and where you are. It is also about the future – where he is going and where you are meant to go. We are not meant to ignore the past, but rather to let the past be transformed. Jesus transformed the cross from an instrument of death and shame into the source of life and glory. With St Paul, we ought to exclaim: "I never boast except in the cross of our Lord Jesus Christ." (Gal 6:14) Jesus transformed the tomb from a place to store the dead into a place from where the dead come back to life. The one who tells you to follow him is the one about whom the disciples said: "On the third day, he rose from the dead." – "We know that Christ, raised from the dead, dies no more. Death no longer has power over him." – "He is risen" – "He is alive."

It is easy to believe in dead ends. That is why so many things are said to be impossible. Many others are said to be difficult. And when they are impossible or difficult, we conclude that there is no way out. Then our lives become impossible and difficult. The bad thing about this type of belief is that it convinces people not only to live in unacceptable situations, but also to contribute actively towards making the situations worse. The result is despair and the loss of hope. People no longer believe in themselves and in their capabilities. We declare that it is fate. We even go so far as to convince ourselves that it is all God's will. If Jesus had left the disciples in the closed room, there would have been no Christianity today.

Your congress had a message – a great message of hope, and of change. Your Jubilee and Congress commitments are clear indications of God's love and trust in you. In God's plan, our Youth, that is you, can and will become more responsible and mature in their lives and styles of life. Among them there will be less irresponsible sex, less dishonesty, less laziness, less aimless living, less drugs, less tribalism, less arrogance towards the elderly. There will be more respect for oneself and for others, more concern for the common good of all, more determination, better use of the meagre resources we have, more unity, more attention to God's Word, more and deeper prayer, and more frequent access to the Sacraments, especially those of the Eucharist and Confession. Are you going to say: "This is impossible"? It will remain impossible only as long as Jesus is absent from your lives. For: "Nothing is impossible for God." (Lk 1:37) "Everything is possible to one who has faith." (Mk 9:23) Dear young people, make now your act of faith and mean it.

The Risen Lord is searching for you now as he did for his disciples. He gave them the Holy Spirit, offered them forgiveness and peace, freed them from the shame of cowardice, filled them with courage and joy and gave them the gift of renewed faith and hope. He removed from their vocabulary the word "impossible". So Jesus searches for you in order to grant you all these gifts of his resurrection.

At the tomb of Lazarus, Jesus asks Martha: "Did I not tell you that if you believe you will see the glory of God?" (Jn 11:40) He told the disciples of Emmaus: "Your story about Jesus, that is me, is correct but incomplete. You have forgotten that this Messiah should suffer these things and so enter into his glory." The story of Jesus will always remain until we believe that he is risen and alive to us. So will our stories remain short and incomplete if we do not

Make now your act of faith and mean it.

believe that he is risen for us. We all need the faith that will enable us to see the glory of God.

The temptation to live and tell uncompleted stories is a real one. Many of our troubles, our sufferings, our mistakes, our worries and fears only speak one language – the language that stops at the cross and lingers around the tomb. The Risen Lord speaks another language, the language of life that continues and renews itself. It is the language that is more powerful than death, sin and evil of all kinds. It is the language that speaks of new life from the grave. It is the language of freedom to be what God wants us to be.

Make your story complete by adding: "Just as Christ was raised from the dead by the glory of the Father, so we too have been raised to live with him in newness of life." (Cf. Rom 6:4). Join Jesus in his victory march. By nature, we are conquerors because we are the children of God. And the victory that conquers the world and our weaknesses is our faith in the Son of God who died and was buried but who rose again from the dead and lives now never to die again.

Dear Young People, believe and you will see the glory of God! That glory shines on the face of our Risen Lord Jesus Christ and will shine on the face of each one of you if you believe.

Happy Easter! Continue moving from victory to victory, from freedom to greater freedom, from holiness to greater holiness. In short, move into newness of life with Jesus.

You are an Easter People and Alleluia is your song.

EASTER MESSAGE 2002

Brothers and Sisters,

The disciples' reaction to the news that Jesus had risen from death was: It has not happened. It will not happen. It cannot happen! – meaning Jesus has not risen, will not, and cannot rise from the dead. From Good Friday, their reaction to Jesus' passion and death was: It should not have happened! It is unbelievable that it happened! Who could ever think it would happen? Why should it have happened that way? They were thinking about Jesus' death on the cross. Yet both the death and the rising happened! They had to accept and to believe both in order to recover their peace of mind and to restore meaning to their lives. So Jesus explained to the two disciples on the road to Emmaus: "Was it not necessary for the Messiah to suffer these things and then to enter his glory?!" (Lk 24:26), and to the other disciples some time later: "This is what is written, the Messiah must suffer and must rise from death three days later..." (Lk 24:46)

Easter is the Passover of the Lord. Christ passed over from death to life as he left this world to return to the Father. His Passover is our Passover. For he affected the Passover also for us, not merely as a future possibility but as a reality here and now, not only for a few but also for every one of us. He made it a way of life for us. He, who called us to take up our cross and follow him, is the Good Shepherd who "calls his sheep by name, leads them out ... and goes before them." (Cf. Jn 10:3-4) In the light of Jesus' resurrection, to follow him means to die and rise with him and to look on his footsteps as a pattern of life.

Jesus gave this wonderful description of his life's work: "The blind can see, the lame can walk, those who suffer from dreaded skin diseases are made clean, the deaf hear, the dead are brought back to life, and the Good News is preached to the poor." (Mt 11:5) He led sinners to repentance and to new life. He gave courage to the fearful, wisdom to the ignorant, and hopes of an eternity of joy with God to all that believe in him. He is "the resurrection and the life" (Jn 14:6), and "the way, the truth and the life". He "is the same yesterday, today and forever." (Heb 13:8)

If this is also our passover, then we must become Passover People, People of the Resurrection. This does not mean living by a vague hope in the good things that will come. It is not a call for us to put on brave faces in difficult times. It means that we develop a new outlook; death does not lead to death, it leads to life. It means faith in Jesus who is risen and alive and who has decided to stay with us always. "I will be with you always to the end of the age." (Mt 28:20) He himself is our hope.

Jesus will never stand by you with his hands folded.

We have a beautiful hymn in Arabic. It goes:

> Let us open our hearts, our lives, our homes so that Jesus may enter. For he comes with salvation for us all:
> Where there is sin, he brings the Good News of Forgiveness
> Where there is sorrow, he brings the Good News of Joy,
> Where there is despair, he brings the Good News of Hope,
> Where there is hatred, he brings the Good News of Love.

And I add:

> Where there are storms, he brings the Good News of Calm.
> Where there is fatigue, he brings the Good News of Rest.
> Where there is illness, he brings the Good News of Healing.
> Where there is death, he brings the Good News of Life.

He will not keep you waiting. He will come in any way, even if the doors are locked. "Just keep believing."

Happy Easter to you all! He is Risen and Alive. Alleluia.

We need to develop a new outlook; death does not lead to death; it leads to life; it means faith in Jesus who is alive.

CHRISTMAS 2003

Brothers and Sisters,

These are days of praise, thanksgiving and joy. We go back to our roots as Christians. We remember an extraordinary event. In this event, God is the principal actor. For God so loved the world that he sent his only Son who was conceived by the power of the Holy Spirit and born of the Virgin Mary. His purpose was to give us life and salvation. We celebrate the first appearance of God on our earth, a man like us. It did not happen by chance. God had planned it from eternity and in the course of human history faithfully and lovingly set himself to realise the plan.

The beauty of Christmas, celebrated each year, is that God continues to realise his plan of salvation. In his Son, we continue to find life, forgiveness, mercy and compassion.

These are all gifts linked to the principal one, namely that the Son of God became flesh so that we might become children of God in and through him. It is a new dignity conferred upon us and is made available for the whole human race. We have been created in the image and likeness of God, but now we are his children.

By becoming man, the Son of God united himself to each and every one of us. That is why we claim that we are children of God. God's Spirit dwells in us - the same spirit that is in the Father and the Son. This places great challenges before us - the challenges we cannot brush off and from which we cannot escape. The challenges are: we are called to be holy because God our Father is holy; to be loving because God our Father is loving; to be merciful and compassionate because God our Father is merciful; to hope and strive for eternal life because God is eternity, and also because it is the right of children to be in the house of their Father.

All this is very good news. But in order to get into its full meaning, we need to reflect on it. We need light to understand and above all to accept its implications.

A last implication I place before you this Christmas is that the good news is for the whole people. It is not a monopoly of Christians. They are obliged by the sheer beauty of the message to bring it to others by word and deed. Our divine worship and our union with Christ make us brothers and sisters to one another, and hands us the task of widening this circle of brothers and sisters. Christmas calls us to live together in love. It is love that shares just as God shared his only Son, his Spirit and life with us. It is love that forgives just as God has forgiven us in Christ. It means being merciful just as God, our Father, is merciful. It contains a strong statement that all human beings are loveable, and capable of responding to love. Out of love flow respect, consideration and appreciation for us and for others. They are attitudes that are offshoots of love and cannot survive without love.

The Holy Father has repeatedly called on the Christian faithful to build a 'civilization of love'. Peace, for which we long so much, can thrive only in an environment of love. It is only love that dissolve the hatred, prolonged anger, envy, greed, pride, violence, injustice and all that render peaceful living impossible. These evils tend to stick to us and to influence all our relationships with one another. They benefit neither those who harbour them nor those towards whom they are directed. They sow bitterness and strife wherever they are found.

Love is an internal force working in all human beings because it has been planted there by God who created them in his image and likeness and transformed them into his daughters and sons in Jesus Christ. He jealously nurtures what he has planted. Christmas is a reminder for us to co-operate with God.

We continuously claim that there is no peace without justice, and rightly so. How much do we realise that there is no greater injustice than that of depriving ourselves and our sisters and brothers of God's greatest gift, the give of LOVE, which is God himself? Our new slogan should now be: "No peace without love". For not even justice can survive without love. This is Christmas!

I wish you all a Happy and Blessed Christmas! I pray that the New Year may be a year of peace cultivated within the "civilisation of love" and supported by love in thought, word and deed.

Subsistence by the Nile.

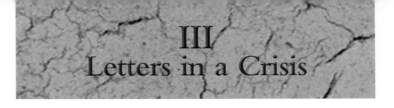

III
Letters in a Crisis

"DO NOT LET EVIL DEFEAT YOU":
ON ANTI-CHRISTIAN PROPAGANDA

Pastoral Letter of Gabriel Zubeir Wako, Archbishop of
Khartoum and of Makram Max Gassis, Bishop of El Obeid,
to their Christian faithful
May 1989

*In the spring and summer of 1989, Sudan was plunged into crisis when,
after only a few years in power, Sadiq al Mahdi was ousted by a coup
d'état. Amid the turmoil, beleaguered Christian communities, especially
those living in Khartoum's notorious displacement camps, were an easy
target for wanton aggression, particularly by extremist Muslim groups. In
this letter to the Archdiocese of Khartoum, the bishops seek to restore calm
and offer the hope of reconciliation. The situation was to remain acutely
problematic long after the political uncertainty was settled when power was
seized by the ruthless General Hassan Omar al-Bashir. President Bashir
was still in power 15 years later when catastrophe hit Darfur, in western
Sudan, where militia fighters killed vast numbers and rendered many more
refugees in their own country and in neighbouring Chad.*

Dear Brothers and Sisters in Christ,
May peace be with you who belong to Christ!

It is the peace of Christ that we wish you. Today, we vividly recall
what Christ did the evening of the day he rose from the dead.
"Jesus came and stood among his disciples. 'Peace be with you,' he
said. After saying this, he showed them his hands and side." (Jn
20:19-20)

1. WHY WE WRITE THIS LETTER

All of you are aware of the sad incidents involving our churches
and faithful. You have heard of the attack on the Church in El
Nuhud (Kordofan, central Sudan).

A similar attack was launched against the Comboni School in Port
Sudan (which overlooks the Red Sea in the north of the country).
On April 21, in Omdurman Church (just outside Khartoum) a
group of men rushed out of a mosque after their Friday prayers
and launched a vicious attack against the Sisters of Mother Teresa
of Calcutta and the patients in their house of care. The assailants
evidently intended to kill the Mother Superior, for they hit her

three times on the head with a club. The Sister fell, but managed miraculously to scramble off to safety.

She could not receive treatment at Omdurman Hospital because the Doctor on duty wanted her to be in the theatre by herself without any Sister to accompany her. The Sister refused. So the doctor dismissed her with a note saying that she had refused treatment.

On April 23, 1989, our prayer centre in El Kamlin (80 miles south east of Khartoum) was burned down.

On April 30, 1989, our centre in Gala'a (Thaura, Omdurman) was set on fire. Our young men managed to put out the fire, but it was too late. Two of the halls were burned down completely. This happened in spite of the promise by the Police to guard the centre. Strangely enough, 27 of the young men who put out the fire were arrested when the Police arrived on the scene.

You are aware of the mounting anti-Christian propaganda being launched from a number of mosques. The position of the Government continues to remain ambiguous. While it condemns the excesses being committed, it adds in the same breath that they are a legitimate "exercise of democracy". The two of us have

Khartoum city centre.

reported all that is happening to the State Minister for the Interior and the Governor of the National Capital. Both men assured us that the Government was taking appropriate measures to curb the growing wave of violence and instigation to violence. We hope that the Government will not wait until more innocent blood is shed.

2. WE NOW ADDRESS YOU

2.1. We appeal to you to keep calm and to refrain from any acts of revenge or violence. No good can come out of violence. So we ask you to maintain your freedom and dignity by refusing to respond to violence and abuse in kind. The aim of these violent groups is to create chaos and to put the government in difficulty. You must not cooperate with them towards such ends.

Besides, you are fully aware that the blame will always be put on you whether you are guilty or innocent. We exhort you therefore to come out of the present crisis with clean hands and hearts.

2.2 We thank God that these troubles have gained momentum in the Season of Easter. We still have fresh memories of Christ's passion, death and resurrection. Let us therefore repeat Christ's prayer on the cross: "Forgive them, Father! They don't know what they are doing." (Lk 23:34) For indeed, where in the world do you see strong, able-bodied men attempting to club an innocent defenceless woman to death? Which culture or religion would incite strong, healthy men to beat up sick people in a house of care? Indeed, those who attacked the Sisters and their patients did not know what they were doing. So we must ask the Father to forgive them. And we must forgive them ourselves.

Before such an example of Christian courage and forgiveness, can any one of you continue to entertain thoughts of revenge and violence?

Sister Joan, the sister who was beaten up, has already given us a splendid example of Christian love and forgiveness. This is what she said to Archbishop Zubeir from her bed of pain: "The Police came this morning to ask me to accompany them to the police station in order to identify my assailants. I told them: "I will not go with you. I don't want you to do anything to those men. Let them go free. Tell them I have forgiven them. Let them go out to continue their Ramadan in peace. Tell them not to attack people any longer." And she continued: "They ask me about the car. You know that the men smashed the windscreens of the car. I told them I could say nothing about the car since it belonged to the Bishop. What shall I tell the Police tomorrow? Please, Bishop, do not raise a case for the car. If you do, I will be obliged to identify those who broke it. I do not want the Police to do anything with those men. Bishop, God help you repair the car." Before such an example of Christian courage and forgiveness, can any one of you continue to entertain thoughts of revenge and violence?

2.3 Do not accuse the Muslims indiscriminately. The violence and insults we experience these days are not the work of all the Muslims but of a particular group. Even common sense can tell you that Islam cannot possibly foment hatred and unwarranted violence! To attack or blame Muslims in general is an act of injustice. You are contributing to the unnecessary suffering of innocent people like you.

2.4 Do not bear hatred or anger against the Muslims who harass you either. Christ's command is clear: "Love your enemies and pray for those who persecute you so that you may become sons of the Father in heaven." (Mt 5:44-45) Our nobility as Christians will be greatly enhanced if we abide faithfully by love's command. We need to listen also to St Paul's exhortation: "Do not let evil defeat you: conquer evil with good." (Rom 12.21)

2.5 You might object: "Are we to allow them to kill us? Will they not take advantage of our goodness?" We must insist with you that our duty as Christians is to prevent the spread of evil. Violence is evil. Yet, we must recall that: "In the name of an elementary requirement of justice, peoples have a right and even a duty to

A class at a 'Save the Saveable' School at Mayo Displacement, Khartoum.

protect their existence and freedom by proportional means against an unjust aggressor."

Clearly, it is primarily the duty of the Government to protect innocent citizens and defuse tensions among the people. For this reason, we deplore the current wrong interpretation of democracy. Democracy is not anarchy. Democracy cannot be maintained in situations of tension. Democracy must be impartial. It cannot grant to certain groups privileges and advantages over others. The democratic right to freely express one's opinion does not give one the right to impose one's opinion on others through violence, terrorism or abuse. Democracy must be based on freedom and respect for all, irrespective of religion and culture. Democracy can survive only where justice for all is guaranteed.

Love and forgiveness are not virtues of cowards but of men of strong religious convictions.

2.6. Believe in the power of love. It is the power of Christ. It is your task as Christ's followers to establish God's kingdom in this country, not by force or deceit but in the power of truth and brotherhood. Do not consider our call for calm as an expression of weakness. We repeat: it is the power of Christ. Before Pilate, Christ declared: "My kingdom is not of this world. If my kingdom belonged to this world, my followers would fight to keep me from being handed over to the Jewish authorities." (Jn 18:36) Love and forgiveness are not virtues of cowards, but of men of strong will and in our case, of strong religious convictions. It is this strength that we call on you to use now.

Dar al Naim displacement camp, Khartoum.

CONCLUSION

The events of these days ought to open our eyes to the miserable condition into which our country has been forced. Unity, brotherhood, cooperation, equality and true freedom have not yet become part of our national heritage. The opposite is true; more effort is being wasted in creating antagonism, in fomenting hatred, in creating divisions and making everyone know that we are not a united nation, or a nation in which all the citizens enjoy equality, freedom and respect.

Christians must realise that they are called to play an important role as peacemakers, promoters of justice and defenders of human dignity and rights. We are called to do this even if we run the risk of being misunderstood.

"To Him who by means of his power working in us is able to do much more than we can ever ask for or even think of: to God be Glory in the Church and in Christ Jesus for all times, for ever and ever! Amen." (Eph 3:20-21)

"THE TRUTH SHALL SET YOU FREE"
THE RIGHTS OF THE CHRISTIAN CITIZENS
A Pastoral Letter of the Bishops of the Sudan
to the Christian faithful
16 November 1991

Little more than two years into Omar al-Bashir's presidency, it was becoming clear that the new regime was every bit as problematic as the bishops of Sudan had feared. A state of emergency had been declared after he came to power and he ruled through a 15-member revolutionary council. By 1991, the Government of Sudan was targeting displaced people arriving in Khartoum to escape the war in the South. Government security forces were bulldozing their homes in the city and forcing them to live in shanty towns with totally inadequate supplies of water, health care and sanitation. It was part of a political Islamisation of society, which was causing alarm to all minority groups, not least the Christians and their bishops.

INTRODUCTION

"May God the Father and Jesus Christ, his Son, give us grace, mercy and peace: may they be ours in truth and love."

The critical situation, which faces the Christian people of the Sudan at the present moment, compels us to write you this joint pastoral letter to our faithful.

Dear brothers and sisters, you, whom God has called us to serve as your Pastors, ask that we speak in support of your efforts to uphold and promote your rights as Christians and free citizens of the Sudan. This is especially true in your right to equal citizenship under the law, your right to the free practice of your religion; your right to defend and preserve your languages and traditional culture and your right as parents to choose the type of education you wish for your children.

We Christians appreciate the fact that we live in a multi-cultural and multi-religious society and thus we respect the fact that Sudanese Christians want to live according to their beliefs. We seek to co-operate with them and with all men and women of good will, in all that generally contributes to the welfare of all citizens. They, like us, seek and work for the realisation of a true, just and lasting peace for our country.

We would like to recall here what was said in the Pastoral letter of the Sudanese Catholic Bishops: "Lord Come to Our Aid" of June 1984. The Bishops appealed to you not to be fearful or confused, to trust that truth will triumph and to defend your faith against false accusations. Such defence is a God-given right. Today, we find ourselves as Christians in very similar circumstances and we wish to encourage you once again to stand firm in your faith.

1. THE PRESENT SITUATION

In spite of repeated public declarations and assurances by the Government that all Sudanese have equal rights; that there is no discrimination based on religion, race, language or culture, we see clearly that the reality is different. It is very evident that present Governmental policies are aimed at creating one nation - a nation that is Islamic in religion and Arab in culture, in total disregard of the large number of Sudanese citizens who are of other faiths and cultures. That such a policy exists is clear to all of us. We wish to highlight some aspects of this policy in support of our claim.

1.1. EDUCATION

I absolve you: A little girl prepares for confession with Fr. Paul Hannon, a former teacher from Newcastle but now a White Father in Hajj Yousif, south of Khartoum.

The Government is openly promoting policies that discriminate against non-Muslim and non-Arab citizens.

a) The heavy emphasis on the use of Arabic as the sole medium for teaching. This policy is being pursued even in schools and areas where, up till now, English has been the medium of instruction. That this policy is against the wishes of many parents and students is clear from the many protests it has provoked. It is clear that this emphasis on Arabic is a means of promoting the Islamisation of the

Sudan. As the Vice President said on 17 September 1991 in connection with the education revolution, Arabic is "like an opening to clearer understanding of the true Islamic roots".

This in itself can be seen as a neutral statement, but when seen in the context of the pressures applied to non-Muslim students to attend Islamic lessons: the official school text books so solidly grounded in Islam and against other faiths; the compulsory school attendance for Christians on Sundays – even in some parts of Southern Sudan: it is clear that Arabic is seen as a means to an end, mainly the Islamisation of the whole student population.

b) The consequence of this policy is the disruption of the studies of those who do not know Arabic, or who don't know it well enough. The total disregard of tribal languages spoken by millions of Sudanese citizens; Fur, Dinka, Nuba, Bari, etc. The need for a national language does not justify the suppression of other languages and as a consequence other cultures.

c) In the field of higher education, the directive from the National Council for Higher Education General Secretariat dated 22 October 1990, that a pass in Islamic Studies be required for entrance into institutes of higher education, clearly shows where the emphasis lies. That the National Council for Higher Education has recently added the words "and other religions" does not really change the original intention to enforce Islamic studies. Our claim that it is so is verified by the statement from H.E. the Minister of Education that "the new educational programme will be a pure Islamic religious educational programme".

d) There is a distortion of truth and reality in the attempts to teach the history of the Sudan as if it began with the coming of Islam. The rich pre-Islamic history – as testified in the National Museum of Khartoum and other places – shows clearly that such a reading of history is incorrect. The idea being proposed that all Sudanese should be taught to respect and revere their "Arab ancestors" makes us ask "What are the Beja, the Hadandawa, the Nuer, the Zande and other tribes to make of such statements?" These people have a rich history of their own which they have a right to study and value.

e) The recent moves to enforce an Islamic dress on all female students is clearly discriminatory.

f) The constant attacks in the mass media on Christian schools and the involvement of the churches in the field of education, causes us concern. Repeated attempts to discredit the major contribution which the churches have made and continue to make to education in the Sudan are clearly unjustified.

We are forced to ask where will such policies lead? Where do such policies leave the non-Arabs and non-Muslim parents when they wish to exercise their rights to determine the sort of education they wish for their children? Where do such policies leave students who are capable of higher education and who wish to exercise their rights to such but who are neither Muslim nor Arab?

Everyone has the right to protect and preserve his or her own cultural identity, his/her language and beliefs. How can this be done under an educational policy, which discriminates in favour of all things Arab and Islamic and against everything non-Arab and non-Muslim?

9.2 ON RELIGIOUS FREEDOM AND FREEDOM OF CONSCIENCE

What sort of citizenship can non-Muslims hope to enjoy under a Government which ignores their existence as free and equal under the law?

a) It is very clear from the mass media, from repeated public statements of Governmental leaders, on the Islamic and Arab identity of Sudan, that non-Arab and non-Muslim citizens are treated only as guests (Zimmi) in their own country. The repeated reference to non-Muslims as "Unbelievers" causes us to ask the question: "What sort of citizenship can they hope to enjoy under a Government which almost ignores their existence as free and equal citizens under the law?"

b) The stress on Islamic Law (Shari'a) as the only legal code for those states which choose Shari'a, still leaves some serious questions unanswered concerning the rights of minorities.

Each state does have its minorities, Christian, Muslim or African Traditional Religion. Both the UN Charter on Human Rights and OAU Charter on Human Rights speak of the absolute need to protect minority rights. We appeal that the principles enshrined in these documents be upheld.

The full application of Shari'a to all citizens in any given State goes against the principles contained in the above charters to which Sudan is a signatory. The argument that the Federal States may choose their own legal code cannot justify ignoring the rights of minorities. The fact that many senior Government positions in the existing states in the South are filled by Muslims appointed by Central Government makes us question the sincerity of the Government's repeated assertion that there will be complete freedom in all States to adopt the system they wish.

We also ask: "How truly representative are the "Popular Committees" of the majority of the citizens in the areas under the committees' control?

c) We wish to see clearly the absolute right of every Muslim to be governed by his or her own legal code (Shari'a). We will always defend this right. We firmly reject the imposition of Islamic law on non-Muslim citizens. For the Government to attempt to apply such laws and enforce them through the use of the State Security Organs is, we maintain, an infringement of its competent authority. We see such composition as a clear violation of the freedom of conscience of the individual, whatever his or her religious belief may be.

As a Christian community, we ask that we be given that same respect for our beliefs, which we firmly believe we must afford the Muslim community. We do not seek confrontation but peace and reconciliation.

We repeat here the clear objection stated by the Bishops in 1984 to "the imposition of the Shari'a Laws on all citizens irrespective of their religion and culture".

Our position has not changed, "Where Shari'a Laws conflict with Christian Tradition and customs and violates the freedom of conscience, you must stand for Christ". ("Lord Come to Our Aid" 1984)

d) The emphasis on Islamisation, Arabization and the implementation of Shari'a Law has very serious consequences for

Christian students in Khartoum.

both freedom of religion and the freedom of conscience of the non-Arab and non-Muslim citizens. We list here some of these consequences:

i) The stopping of any Christian preaching in the area of Damazin (in eastern Sudan); the expulsion of the Parish Priest from Damazin; the attempted confiscation of Church land and property in Damazin town.

ii) The arbitrary arrest and detention of the Priest and catechists in Dongola (250 miles north of Khartoum).

iii) The expulsion of all missionary personnel from South Kordofan (central Sudan, centring on the politically disputed Nuba mountains).

iv) The closure and destruction of Church centres among the displaced citizens in El Obeid and Khartoum.

v) The repeated refusal in many areas to issue building permits for churches and church centres.

vi) The attempt to equate the Christian Churches with Western or foreign power.

vii) Accusation in the Government-controlled press that the Church "spreads poison" in the minds of the people, and that the Church is anti-Islamic.

viii) All of you are aware of the constant harassment of priests, sisters and lay Christians by members of the Security Forces.

ix) The pressure applied to non-Muslims in some prisons to convert

A people of prayer: Inside the church in Hajj Yousif, south of Khartoum.
Photo: A. Polec.

to Islam with the promise of being set free and being given money if they do convert.

x) The introduction of questions on Islam in interviews for work with the government, and the requirement that job applicants produce a legal testimonial that they are Muslims. We know of two young Christian men who failed the interview because of these requirements.

xi) The obvious use in some places of "food aid" to promote Islam. The move to place the displaced people in such a situation of distress through preventing them receiving aid and then allowing Islamic NGOs to offer assistance to them.

The few examples we have given above are the clear indication of the anti-Christian actions that are a direct result of Government policy. You are familiar with these cases and, no doubt, could cite many more examples. The Government cannot claim that these are all isolated incidents resulting from over-zealous officials acting without proper authority. Such officials would not behave as they do unless convinced that they had the backing of a higher authority. If the government allows the Press, Radio and TV - all of which are state-controlled - to abuse constantly and attack non-Arab and non-Muslim citizens, then the Government is morally responsible for the consequences. Such attacks engender an atmosphere of fear, distrust and even hatred. We ask: "Is the Government serious in its claim to be creating a new order - where freedom and respect for all religions is to be found; that Sudan is a multi-religious society?"

If it is serious then let it put an immediate end to all these public abuses of the rights of non-Arab and non-Muslim citizens.

We wish to state clearly that the present policy of Islamisation and Arabization being followed by the Government can only lead to disharmony and place obstructions on the road to a true, just and lasting peace in the Sudan.

2. THE LIGHT OF FAITH

"God made man imperishable; he made him in the image of his own nature." (Wisdom 2:23)

It is our belief that we judge the present situation in the light of faith. Our faith teaches us that as we are created in God's image and that our very humanity is blessed by Christ taking upon himself our human nature. (Phil 2) We are compelled by faith to protect and promote the dignity of every man and woman. Our concern for human rights, freedom and truth is a religious concern based on faith. We are therefore urged to help all people to understand this

We are compelled to help all in the struggle to be fully human, with full rights and liberties under a just law.

truth. We are compelled to help all in the struggle to be fully human, with full rights and liberties under a just law. We seek to protect the good of all and are happy and willing to do so with our fellow citizens of the Muslim faith, in friendship and dialogue. We recall some further words from the Bishops' 1984 letter: "That dignity and basic equality of all are the foundations of justice. That is why we call on you to stand for justice and for your rights. Do not fail to enter into dialogue with those who think and act differently from you. Raise your complaints without fear. Use any democratic and legal means available. Only, be careful not to tread on other people's rights while demanding yours." ("Lord Come to our Aid")

We wish to end this section with an appeal to Government and to all men and women of good will. Let us work together for the promotion of all that will bring real peace and unity in our beloved nation. Let us do what we can to promote the rights of all citizens. Only then can we begin to live in harmony and peace.

3. OUR RESPONSE TO THE PRESENT SITUATION

"The truth shall make you free." (Jn 8:32)

We wish to encourage all of you to respond in faith, truth and love. We quote again from the Bishops' Letter of 1984. "We repeat: using Christ's weapons of love, forgiveness, patience and understanding does not imply that you give in to injustice. You have to stand for the truth at all times, the truth about yourselves in that you are citizens of this country like anyone else with equal rights to be respected and benefit from what the State makes available, and equal rights to participate fully in the life of the country. There is the truth that you are Africans and Christians, and therefore have the right to live in this country according to your culture, customs and religion. These are your rights, not only as citizens but also as human beings. There is the truth about the other citizens: they have the right to be different. They have the right to live according to their customs, culture and religions, but absolutely no right to impose their customs and religion on you. You owe them respect and understanding, because these are indispensable for life together. The truth about yourselves and about others imposes mutual obligations, if you are to live in the same country. We have already mentioned the fundamental obligations of mutual respect, mutual understanding and mutual recognition of each other's rights and duties."

What therefore can we do?

3.1. Be united to Christ at all times. Work to create an atmosphere of love and respect.

3.2. Be prepared to defend your rights. In this matter, we support the positive and peaceful actions of the Christians in Damazin: we support those parents and students who peacefully demand that their voice be heard. We say, be firm, be courageous, be non-violent.

3.3. We appeal to Christian parents: be aware of your God given right to nourish your children in those beliefs and traditions you hold sacred. Education in such things is all the more important at this time within the family, when your children are constantly exposed to other values alien to your beliefs and traditions.

3.4. We appeal to the Christian community at the Parish and Centre level to reflect on your communities the real Gospel values of love and peace. Be places where true human rights can be found. Study together how to live God's word in your communities. Look at your situation – judge it in the light of faith; act according to this faith judgement at all times. Form truly Christian communities, supportive of one another, where no one suffers alone or rejoices alone, where our sense of love and solidarity for one another can truly enlighten and liberate those who hold wrong ideas about us.

3.5. We appeal to all pastoral workers: Priests, Sisters, Catechists, to help the Christian community to be aware of its God given rights, and to help it to defend these rights at all times. We appeal for prayer that all may see God's hand at work in the present situation and strive for the coming of the kingdom of peace and love.

3.6. We appeal to the Christian leaders in Government: you are the yeast to transform policies in order to promote peace and justice, respect for human rights, honesty and truth. Your position lays on you a heavy responsibility, you are called to be an example to others. Put the common good above personal gain. Your failure to speak for what is right and true may lead to greater suffering among your own people. Be courageous and faithful in your call from God to save the people.

3.7. We appeal to the Christian youth. You will build the future. You are told very often that you are the future. Ask yourselves the question: "What sort of future do you want?" Do not be afraid to state your answer clear in the light of the Gospel. Be truthful and honest; be brave and loving: be firm in your faith; build up your strength in union with Christ. Be constant in prayer and always support one another. Study the Gospel and the teaching of the Church so that you may defend your faith with confidence and knowledge. Form study and prayer

Be courageous and faithful in your call from God to save the people.

groups to nourish your faith. Always respect your own dignity as sons and daughters of God.

CONCLUSION

We are not alone.

"I am with you to the end of time." (Mt 28:20)

We are sometimes faithful, we are sometimes unsure, we are sometimes deeply worried about the future. But we believe in Christ and live in hope. We have faith in the triumph of good over evil. Let us love and trust one another. Let us be courageous as we try to build for the future. Let us pray constantly for peace and justice. We, your pastors, having spoken to you these words of hope and encouragement, ask for your prayer that we may continue, together with you to strive fearlessly for the promotion of all that will build a future of justice, love and peace for all Sudanese.

+ Gabriel Zubeir Wako, Archbishop of Khartoum
+ Vincent Mojwok Nyeker, Bishop of Malakal
Msgr Rudolph Deng Majak, Apostolic Administrator of Wau
Very Rev. Boutros Kuku Trille, Vicar General of El Obeid

TO THE CHRISTIAN FAITHFUL IN DAMAZIN
Pastoral Letter of Gabriel Zubeir Wako, Archbishop of Khartoum
28 November 1991

A 500-mile journey from Khartoum, Damazin, in eastern Sudan, was the unlikely venue for a flashpoint in the Christian struggle for religious freedom. In the early 1990s, when Sudan's President Bashir was mounting a concerted, ruthless attack on all forms of possible opposition, the Parish Priest of Damazin was falsely accused of collusion with the rebels. What followed showed just how much the Christian community had to fear from the worst of Islamic extremism. In a letter intended to restore calm, the Archbishop pays tribute to the courage of faith of a Christian community tested as never before. True to form, he finds a glimmer of Christian hope amid the darkness of despair and urges his faithful to be people of forgiveness, not anguish and self-righteous fury.

Dear Brothers and Sisters,

"We wish you the grace and peace of God, our Father and of the Lord Jesus Christ". (Phil 1:2) These are my greetings and the greetings of the whole Archdiocese of Khartoum, who have been very close to you during the trials you all went through at the beginning of this month.

And this is Jesus Christ, "the first and the last, who was dead and has come to life again", speaking to you. "I know the trials you have had". (Rev 2:9) Yes, he knows and he tells you: "Do not be afraid of the sufferings that are coming to you... Even if you have to die, keep the faith and I will give you the crown of life for your prize." (Rev 2:10)

At the beginning of this month of November, the Commissioner of Damazin ordered the priest of your Parish to hand him all the keys of the parish homes. Rumours spread that the Commissioner intended to turn the Parish premises into a Police Station, "because there was no Church in Damazin". When the news reached you, all of you; men, women and children, abandoned your homes and flocked into the parish compound to await the day of the take-over. Reports that reach me say you spent whole nights in prayer together. In those days you lived in almost perfect unity, with one mind and purpose: "they will take over these premises over our dead bodies." The appointed day came. Nothing happened.

1. LET US JUDGE WHAT HAPPENED.

All your brothers and sisters in the faith have greatly appreciated the stand you took, the unity that brought you together and the determination you showed. It was not only the Church that you defended but also the honour of our country, for the take-over of the parish premises would have been a breach of justice, that would have attracted international attention. One would have expected the Commissioner to contact the authorities of the

When the news reached you, all of you abandoned your homes and flocked into the parish compound. You spent whole nights in prayer together.

A Khartoum priest with children in a displacement camp.

Church in Khartoum since these plots were bought by them. There was no need of hurry to take over these buildings.

You gave a concrete example of how the poor and the weak can stand up for their rights if they are united. You relied on prayer, that is, God's protection. You opened a new page of being Church in our Archdiocese, completely breaking with the old custom when you would have all run to Khartoum to ask the Bishop to go to save you. You gave an example of Church that is gradually acquiring its identity and internal strength.

The Commissioner, in spite of the unjust order he had given to take over our premises, nevertheless proved to be a man of judgement. We ought to express to him our appreciation. For he reversed, or at least suspended, his decision when he saw that it would cause unrest and unnecessary bloodshed. Someone else in his place would have resorted to force in order to show his power. This man, however, knew how to read "the signs of the times". To appreciate better the action of Commissioner, we need to recall that a month before, he expelled the Parish Priest of Damazin, Fr De Bertolis, on the grounds that "there was no Church in Damazin, so he had no more reason to stay in Damazin". The Immigration and Passports Office ordered the Father to leave the town within 72 hours. Then the Commissioner ordered the Sisters not to set foot in the kindergartens run by the Church and had a Muslim lady take charge of the kindergartens. He moved to order the Sudanese resident priests in Damazin to stop any Christian "preaching" in Damazin since there was no Church there. Then the final blow came when he decided to take over the Church premises and presumably expel the Sudanese priests from Damazin.

Photo: A. Polec

After all such steps, it must have taken him much courage to reverse at least temporarily his decision. For the time being, I call this wisdom and understanding. I thank the Commissioner for saving the lives of so many people and for saving our country from being an area of religious wars and conflicts.

Our greatest thanks and praise to God, who gave you courage to stand together for what is right and just, who gave the Commissioner the wisdom and right to withdraw at least temporarily his decision and who saved all of you from violence and death. To God be praise and glory for ever and ever!

2. AND NOW?

Be on the watch out.

All through this letter, I have hinted that the decision not to take over the Church has merely been a temporary measure. For this reason, you need to keep on the watch so that you may not be taken by surprise. This means you have to continue talking with the local authorities about the seriousness of the steps they are preparing to take. Your right as Christian citizens is to have your place of worship.

We have been requesting a permit to have a church in Damazin since 1969. In order to keep the authorities from forgetting the request, we applied twice a year for all these 22 years. All we managed to obtain was a permit to run kindergartens and to hold evening classes. In 1981, the town council showed me the plan of Damazin town. In it, there was a plot for the church. Two years later, I consulted the same map and the name of the church was no longer there. I asked why. I was told that the original site for the church had been put to other uses but that I could obtain another site if I applied for it. I applied for the succeeding years and nothing came of it. This is a clear indication that the plan not to give a place for worship to Christians is an old plan which the present Administration of Damazin intends to execute. They have however gone further than that by deciding to take over even the house I built with all the required permits as residences for priests and sisters and on plots I purchased.

3. NO VIOLENCE OR HATRED.

I came to know that some of you were preparing to meet violence with violence. The Lord's command to you is: "Love your enemies and pray for those who persecute you. In this way, you will be sons of your Father in heaven, for he makes his sun to rise on bad as well as good, and his rain to fall on honest and dishonest alike."

(Mt 5: 44-45) Therefore, NO VIOLENCE, NO INSULTS, NO THOUGHTS OF REVENGE, NO HATRED because we are disciples of Christ. Our programme in this country is that of building a NEW AND A MORE HUMAN CIVILIZATION based on the Gospel: the civilization of love, of mutual understanding among people, of respect for every human person, of reconciliation given and received, of justice for all and peace. We cannot bring about such a civilization if we allow other people to lead us into the ways of violence, hatred and revenge.

The call of non-violence does not mean you have to let people walk all over you. When you defend your rights and dignity, you defend the dignity and honour of God.

The call to NON VIOLENCE does not mean you have to lie down and let people walk over you. You have to remember your dignity as images and children of God. When you defend your rights and dignity, you defend the dignity and honour of God. But God does not want his dignity to be defended with wars and violence. He who does violence to his fellow man, or acts unjustly against his brothers and sisters, lowers his or her own dignity, particularly if he uses such violence against those whom he considers weaker than himself. In our African traditions, there is no word of praise for a big man who fights a child or someone who does not match him in strength and size or does not hold the same kind of weapon he or she uses in the attack. As Pope John Paul II says: violence degrades man; and violence is un-Christian. We should not accept such degradation.

Always stand for your rights, but in a NON VIOLENT way. What you are looking for is not the destruction of others, but the preservation of your rights and dignity. Violence must be the very, very last resort reserved almost specifically for self-defence, when any other means including the dignified retreat becomes impossible.

You have realised that in UNITY there is strength, strength to encourage one another, and strength to challenge unwarranted attacks. Your unity is a great form of non-violent resistance. But above all, if you come together in Christ's name and keep together in his name, THERE HE IS IN YOUR MIDST.

4. CONCLUSION

I wish now to share some reflections in one of the homilies of St John Chrysostom:

Jesus said to his disciples: "Remember, I am sending you out like sheep among wolves so be cunning as serpents and yet as harmless as doves." (Mt 10:16)

So long as we continue to behave as sheep, we are victorious. Even if 10,000 wolves surround us, we conquer and are victorious. BUT THE MOMENT WE BECOME WOLVES, WE ARE CONQUERED, FOR WE LOSE THE HELP OF THE SHEPHERD. Christ is the shepherd of sheep, not of wolves. This is what Jesus confirmed to Paul: "My grace is sufficient for you, for my power is made perfect in weakness."

But the Lord continues: "Be cunning (wise) as serpents and innocent (harmless) as doves." We may ask: "How can we have wisdom at all when we are deluged by such billows? However wise sheep may be when in the midst of wolves, if wolves are as numerous as they are what more will wisdom be able to achieve? However innocent the doves may be, what advantage will their innocence be when so many hawks beset them?" The answer is that we are human beings and not really serpents and doves, so as human beings in such situations, we can obtain the greatest advantages. The wisdom of the serpent in danger is this: it abandons everything, even if its body has been cut off, and does not resist much, provided only it can save its head. In the same way Christ says: abandon everything except your faith, even if it means giving up your wealth, your body, or your life itself. Your faith is your head and your roots.

Jesus tells us to continue wisdom and innocence; wisdom, so as not to receive mortal wounds: and innocence, so as not to take revenge against those who do us harm, nor bear a grudge against those who plot against us. Wisdom is no use by itself unless there is innocence as well.

Christ knows that: VIOLENCE IS NOT OVERCOME BY VIOLENCE, BUT BY FORBEARANCE, that is patience, Christian forgiveness, reconciliation, peace and LOVE.

Thank you for the witness you have given our Church. Thanks for your courage. Thanks for your unity.

To God, from whom all good things come, be glory and praise and thanksgiving, FOR EVER and EVER. Amen

+ Gabriel Zubeir Wako
Archbishop of Khartoum

*A fearless faith:
Fr. Guido*

Damazin: – Fr Guido Ganji

A Priest's Memories of the Damazin disaster

FR GUIDO GANJI was at the heart of the crisis that erupted in Damazin.

Sent there shortly after being ordained by Archbishop Zubeir Wako, he was appointed assistant to the parish priest of Damazin, Fr De Bertolis.

Within a month of Fr Guido's arrival in Damazin, Fr De Bertolis was forced out of the area by the regional authorities.

Recalling the incident with crystal clear freshness more than a dozen years later, Fr Guido remembered how the district commissioner demanded that the church keys be handed over. "I told him," said Fr Guido, "I would never give him the keys. I then went to the people and told them: "This is your place. You are Sudanese. You have a right to be in this place no matter what."

Under Fr Guido's leadership, the people gathered in the church day and night for 72 hours or more. "I put up a big cross at the church," said Fr Guido. "I rang the bells through the night. We all prayed together in the church."

Fr Guido campaigned vigorously to save the church and his efforts eventually won him an interview with President Bashir himself. Fr Guido was given three months to build another church after which time his old one would have to make way for the police station the regional authorities wanted to put in its place.

"They never expected me to build the church in the time available," recalls Fr Guido. Charitable support provided key funding for the new church and with the hands-on help of so many parishioners, the building work was completed within the allotted period. Fr Guido smiled with pride as he recalled that the new church was built with a seating capacity of 400.

The experience, so early on in Fr Guido's ministry, was a seminal moment for the young priest, who is now Episcopal Vicar for the Clergy in the Archdiocese of Khartoum, helping priests in difficult situations. "I had a very hard situation to face in Damazin," he said, "and it means I am in a good position to give a lot of help and encouragement to priests who face hardships today."

INTER-RELIGIOUS DIALOGUE IN THE SUDAN - CAN WE SUSTAIN IT?

A talk by His Grace Archbishop Gabriel Zubeir Wako
during the Conference on Inter-religious Dialogue
Khartoum, 5 October 1994

*"The Truth Will Set You Free". This is Cardinal Zubeir Wako's motto as
Archbishop and, throughout his episcopate, he has never sought to conceal
the full gravity of the grievances against Christian communities at the
hands of political Muslim extremists: the demolition of churches, the attacks
on Church-run "Save the Saveable" schools, the anti-Christian propaganda
in the government-run media. The list goes on. But it is a mark of
Cardinal Zubeir Wako's pastoral sensitivity that he has seized upon every
opportunity for reconciliation, not out of defeatist compromise but with a
firm conviction that true peace can be won in a way that benefits both
sides. Speaking as President of the Sudan Bishops' Conference, he
addresses a meeting called by the Government of Sudan and attended by
major religious leaders.*

Mr Chairman,
Your Excellencies,
Ladies and Gentlemen,

**May God the Father and the Lord Jesus Christ give you
the grace and peace.**

The purpose of this paper is to convince myself that there are
good prospects for a lasting inter-religious dialogue in the Sudan
and among the Sudanese People.

Photo: A. Polec

1. THE "HERE"

In the Sudanese situation I think it is a big mistake and a blind disregard of reality to consider and present our "here" as a peaceful and neutral paradise of religious tolerance, inter-religious harmony, and peaceful coexistence. Arguments that idealise our situation by comparing it to that prevailing in other countries are doing the country a disservice. One cannot disregard a case of plague in the Sudan simply because it is nothing compared to the epidemic in India. Wrong is determined by its wrongness, not by its prevalence.

Wrong is determined by its wrongness, not by its prevalence.

1.1 How the Christian sees our "HERE"

The normal Christian looks at this very Conference with scepticism: "Then they are at it again", meaning, we are out again to deceive the world and ourselves. The Christian believes in dialogue, believes in the benefits accruing to it, believes that it is a duty. He believes also that dialogue in the Sudanese situation calls into play some of the Gospel values that Jesus Christ vigorously inculcated into his followers: mutual forgiveness, patience, humility, meekness, charity, hope and faith in the power of God, and faith in the reconciling power of Christ's death on the cross. Why then is he sceptical about dialogue? One reason is that several attempts in the past have failed. Another is that dialogue in the other vital areas in the life of the nation have made no headway, e.g. the dialogue for peace and an end to the civil war … Yet another is that real trust has broken down between the two communities, and, what looks like trust, is a manoeuvre for survival for both communities.

In the light of all these, the ordinary Christian defines our "here" as a here of religious tensions, conflicts and uncertainties, the uncertainties being more pronounced for the Christian. The Christian who thinks this way is the one who feels discriminated against at school, in the work place, in the army and even in

The Sudanese way of life: Hajj Yousif, south of Khartoum.

housing and social services. He is the one who feels his right to freedom of worship is curtailed, when he cannot have a decent place to pray in, or cannot gather his fellow Christians to pray in his house on some family occasions, or loses his job because the interview includes questions from the Holy Koran, which he never dreamt of learning. At the same time, there is the Christian who claims that everything is all right and that what the ordinary Christian fears or complains about is nothing but deliberate anti-Sudanese propaganda. For this class of Christian, there is not even need for dialogue because dialogue already exists.

1.2. How the Muslim sees our "HERE"

Muslims also seem to be divided on the issue of dialogue. There are those who sincerely feel that things are not all right, those who feel that Christians, particularly those from the South, are discriminated against and maltreated on religious grounds, and who even openly express their sympathy. This group of Muslims strongly advocates dialogue. Their understanding of the "here" is that situations of tension do exist, and that such tensions, especially where religion is at stake, will in the long run break up the nation, alienate groups of citizens, create a situation of chaos, and lower the value of religion itself. They believe that God is one, and only one for all and the Father of all, and that all human beings are brothers and sisters. Some others, those who feel that the Sudan is and must remain an Islamic country, want to see that everything be Islamic, that no other religion be mentioned except Islam, and that everyone who claims to be Sudanese should bow before Islamic values whether he/she understands them or not. This group believes there is no possibility of dialogue with "Kuufar", and even question the morality of the Muslim who engages in such a dialogue. This group has gained some ascendancy of late. The bulk of the Sudanese, tired of living under constant tension, strongly opts for dialogue, not only between Muslims and Christians but also between the various regions, cultures and ethnic groups in the Sudan. Most Sudanese hold firm the principle of good neighbourliness. "A good neighbour is a blessing from God."

1.3 An informed public opinion is indispensable for the departure from "here"

An initiative for dialogue therefore demands a multi-faceted programme of awareness-raising, to unify the Christian and Muslim ranks even in the idea of starting some kind of dialogue, let alone in tackling the more crucial issues that also need to be treated once the spirit of real dialogue has permeated our society. This is why I have always insisted that our main effort now should be that of creating awareness in our communities, of the need for dialogue, understanding and harmony among the followers of the various religions; that of accepting the diversity among us even in religious matters as blessings from God to our nation. Such diversity often challenges the depth of our own faith. Our people need to be educated to accept one another just as we are, to respect one another, and within the object of this respect, to include the different ways if thinking, the languages, the cultures and their expression. We need to promote this diversity, because in promoting it we promote the human persons immersed in it, and that is promoting the "image and likeness of God" in which all human beings are created. And since followers of some of the great world religions believe that they are commissioned by God to propagate their faith, we need to convince one another that conversion to faith, that is, in terms of a deeper faith commitment is, in the final analysis, a very personal affair. It is a matter of personal conviction and of conscience, the human conscience, which may not be violated or subjected to force, coercion, deceit, or manipulation. After all, these acts should be considered affronts to God, who in calling human beings to believe in Him, to serve and worship Him, does not accept the worship of slaves. He wants them to be free human beings who come to Him freely in response to truth and goodness, because He endowed each of them with that divine attribute which we call freedom. As I said in the February meeting of the Pontifical Council for Inter-religious Dialogue: "Both Christians and Muslims must renew their faith in the power of God who is almighty. God does not need human beings to fight for Him. He can fight and win his own battles."

The suffering Church: Khartoum priest Fr. Charles with children outside a chapel in a displacement camp.

2 HOW DO WE MOVE FROM "HERE"?

2.1 Honest acceptance of the "here

"The dialogue we need in the Sudan demands radical changes in our approach to problems. The Sudanese are prone to accept disturbing situations with a "ma'alesh" (Arabic for "don't worry"). Such an attitude towards problems is helpful, but it has a tendency of leaving problems untouched until their next recurrence. The Sudanese dialogue will begin to take a turn for seriousness when all those involved honestly accept the existence of unresolved tensions and conflicts, the existence of divisive and discriminating political and social policies, the existence of built-up frustrations, resentments and anger, an abundance of prejudices and suspicions ... and everything which can make even the prospects for dialogue a mere day dreaming. That is why I have always opposed those who claim that the Sudanese are by nature a tolerant people open to dialogue, and that in the Sudan there exists no type of religious tension or discrimination. Those who say this are only partially right, though we might say they are afraid. For to accept that there are religious tensions would place the Sudan among countries that are disrespectful of human rights. My own vision of the situation is that the religious issue together with its racial counterpart is part and parcel of all the tensions that have marred our recent history, or, more appropriately, they have been induced in order to sharpen the tensions. We have further to note that what causes tension between people could be real or imaginary; but, real or imaginary, they need to be honestly tackled and reassessed before it blows out of control.

Whatever causes tension - real or imaginary - needs to be tackled before it blows out of control.

2.2 The need for confrontation

In dialogue it is not enough to search for objectivity. For pain can generate quarrels and discontent. I, therefore, suggest that our quest for dialogue must encourage those who feel pinches, those who feel uncomfortable with the way others treat them, become more vocal and confront those who cause these pinches. Forums should be created for them to voice their troubles freely and without fear. Their confrontation should be determined and persevering, but non-aggressive and non-judgemental. It does not help to blame, shame or attack. All of us need to bear in mind that a problem is not a complaint. A difficulty is not a complaint. Persons and groups of persons should be free to expose their problems and difficulties. The others, at least out of courtesy, have the duty to listen.

2.3 Dialogue, like peace, is impossible without justice

We need also to look carefully into structures that are taken for granted and are considered unchangeable. I tried to tackle one of these and someone told me I was going political. I asked: "Are we then to consider that the dialogue ends here?" "No, but we should avoid political issues. We are religious leaders." If religious leaders cannot tackle unjust structures, who is going to? How are they going to preach a just God, without calling on human beings to become just as their Heavenly Father is just? My question has not yet been answered. Religion cannot be lived in a vacuum. We have to convince ourselves that elements foreign to religion often need religion for their survival. It is the scripture saying that the devil can disguise himself as the angel of light. Wherever religion enters, it must bring the light of God even if that means bitter confrontation with the angels of darkness.

2.4 Dialogue must be at the service of the common good of all

Dialogue aims at removing suspicion, division, prejudices and confrontation. In this way, it promotes solidarity and co-operation among people. The object of dialogue is the common good of all, and the inalienable rights of every human being. This statement rules out the dictatorship of the majority, because the common good includes the good of the minority, and the inalienable rights of every human being as an individual person. One of the main pursuits of our dialogue should therefore be a search for what unites Muslims and Christians. These should first be well established before we face the divisive issues. Such a procedure comes out of the conviction that "the welfare of a people can never be accomplished in opposition to the welfare of another" – and – "neither the common good nor peace can ever be constructed by some without the others."

Wherever religion enters, it must bring the light of God even if that means bitter confrontation with angels of darkness.

2.5 Dialogue must be persevering

Dialogue must be persevering. It is a difficult exercise. One reason is that it is an exercise in which all parties should emerge as winners. In real dialogue there are no losers, neither may losers be created without dealing a deathblow to dialogue itself. Persons in dialogue should not allow themselves to be discouraged by real or apparent failures. They should consent to begin again ceaselessly to propose true dialogue, by removing obstacles and eliminating the defects of dialogue ... and travel to the end of this single road which leads to peace with all its demands and conditions.

As Pope John Paul II said: "To give up on dialogue is to lose faith in man, the human being." We must continue to preserve enough confidence in man, in his capacity of being reasonable, in his sense of what is good, of justice, of fairness, in his possibility of brotherly love and hope...

2.6 Dialogue needs action

Dialogue must lead to action. "Dialogue that remains for ever on the level of theory, discussions and exchange of ideas cannot be called meaningful. It should always end with some concrete programmes of common action. This is simply because tensions, quarrels, wars do not happen only at the level of words; sooner or later the hard words will turn into blows and other undesirable physical acts. Only action will undo action." (Sudanese Catholic Bishops' Pastoral Letter: "Lend Me Your Ears")

The action programme for our dialogue should, I believe, include the following:

A. Creating awareness in the public of existing situations of religious intolerance and the need of ongoing dialogue and the demands of such a dialogue. Such an awareness should lead the citizens to agree to only one form of intolerance: intolerance towards intolerance particularly in what concerns religious freedom and practice.

B. Educating the public to respect and accept those who do not think or act as themselves; examining our present political and social policies and structures with a view to drawing the attention of the responsible authorities to any aspects that could generate tensions, create misunderstandings, or put sections of the population into permanent difficulties.

C. Requesting that the competent authorities set up forums to hear the difficulties and problems of citizens, especially in matters that touch the freedom of worship and religious practice, and to follow up towards solving those problems.

The garment of righteousness: Traditional African clothes being made with antique British 'Singer' sewing machines. Jaborora displacement camp, outside Khartoum.

D. Organising in-depth studies or conferences to enable Muslims and Christians to understand and even challenge one another's understanding of issues such as: the meaning of freedom of religion and of worship; the role of religion in politics and society and how to reconcile diverse religious views in these matters; the application of religious laws like the Islamic Shari'a on people who do not adhere to that particular faith; the dialogue for peace to end the ongoing civil war and to create an atmosphere conducive to peace and brotherhood among the Sudanese People ... (It is my belief that if these issues are not politicised, but addressed in order to understand better what people of different religions and cultural traditions think on them, such studies could be of great benefit to all). Then the other proposals listed in the constitutions of the Council for Inter-religious Dialogue could be followed and realised.

CONCLUSION

Finally, to return to the question which I began; I believe that dialogue between Christians and Muslims is possible, and that we are able to live together as brothers and sisters. However, this conviction can only become a reality if:

1) The Council for Inter-religious Dialogue is considered and supported by all citizens and authorities, as a long-awaited forum to end a situation that was going to drive the country into chaos, examining our present political and social policies and structures with a view to drawing the attention of the responsible authorities to any aspects that could generate tensions, create misunderstandings or put sections of the population into permanent difficulties.

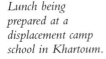

Lunch being prepared at a displacement camp school in Khartoum.

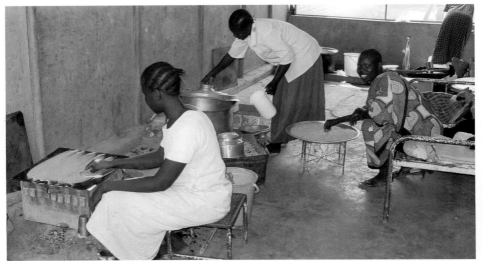

2) The Council for Inter-religious Dialogue takes its responsibilities seriously, and its members are prepared to take the risks involved in a programme as delicate as this.

3) The whole process of dialogue is taken seriously with the determination to make it work in practice, and not merely as window dressing to deceive international public opinion and ourselves.

4) Our country renews its Faith in God, and trusts that in his providence he will not allow his children to go on for ever hurting and destroying one another, instead of standing together to build and support one another in the spirit of brotherly solidarity that expands particularly towards those of them who stand most in need of care and support.

+ Gabriel Zubeir Wako
Archbishop of Khartoum

VISION, MISSION AND VALUES FOR A RENEWED COMMITMENT TO PEACE IN THE SUDAN

Pastoral Letter of the Catholic Bishops of the Sudan
to the Christian Faithful and
to all Persons of Goodwill in the Sudan
8 September 1997

By the late 1990s, the Government of Sudan and the rebels in the south had been slogging it out in a gruesome blood bath that had been running for 15 years or more. Both sides were entrenched in positions of no compromise. Much-heralded signs of peace too often came to nothing. The death toll now ran into millions and Khartoum and its environs were quickly filling up with bedraggled orphans of war, escapees from the conflict in the south. Would this nightmare ever end? It was easy to be jaundiced but in a bid to rouse themselves from weary resignation to the status quo, the bishops decided to set out their "Vision for Sudan". Unequivocal, uncompromising and undimmed in its apostolic zeal, the letter sets out once and for all that peace and justice remain the twin goals of the bishops and that their hearts should not rest until these two pillars of civilisation are firmly set in place.

PRESENTATION

Brothers and Sisters,
Grace and Peace to you.

The word "Peace" has become the most spoken word in our country today. We all want and long for peace. The future of our country and the happiness of our people will depend on the kind of peace we reach.

There is the peace of death. There is the "peace" one experiences after the total extermination of one's enemies. There is the peace in which no guns are fired but in which people are trodden underfoot, despised, discriminated against and are made very unhappy. There is the peace in which people do not talk to one another, "the peace of the dumb", because people hate and fear one another, because there is selfishness, greed, pride, and so many other "walls" they have built between themselves.

The Catholic bishops of the Sudan during their annual plenary assembly in Rome (September 1997) reflected on all these kinds of peace and said: "None of them is peace, none can be called peace". Indeed we need peace that is worthy of human beings and enjoyed by everyone. No human being will exert his/her energies for meaningless peace.

We looked at the terrible situation of non-peace in the Sudan. It was frightful and detestable. So we asked ourselves: "What kind of peace does the Sudan need today?" Not just any peace, but the kind of peace for which people are prepared to struggle, to spend their energies and even to die.

This is how our VISION FOR THE SUDAN was born. From now on, we will not just be working for the Sudan but for the kind of Sudan we saw in our VISION - our vision of a better and happier Sudan. In our present situation such a vision of the Sudan

> We need peace worthy of human beings and enjoyed by everyone. No human being will exert his/her energies for meaningless peace.

A Sanctuary for the Suffering: Inside the parish compound at Hajj Yousif, south of Khartoum.

seems a dream precisely because there are so many forces working in the opposite direction.

Our MISSION STATEMENT spells out our programme of work to weaken the forces of evil and strengthen those of good. It is our commitment. It is the very mission Jesus Christ took upon himself, and handed on to his disciples for all times. Such a Mission Statement is demanding.

So, we set before ourselves certain VALUES to sustain us in our effort. These values are based on Christian faith, hope and love. They must become integral to our Christian Vocation and Ministry as Bishops. They are values that should help and urge us to reach out imploringly to God with whom nothing is impossible. They have to be cultivated with patience and perseverance until they become second nature to us.

We now share our VISION, STATEMENT AND VALUES with you. Our hope is that they become the "Vision, Mission and Values of the Church in the Sudan" as it struggles together with all Sudanese of good will to restore peace to our country.

We ask you to pray for us, your Bishops, that we may continue to be light and salt in our country. We ask you to gradually make our "Vision, Mission and Values" your very own. Through the intercession of Mary, our Mother, of Blessed Bakhita and Blessed Comboni, we shall and will obtain from God all the graces we need to bring peace to our country.

Brothers and Sisters, we have a very noble programme to work, suffer and even die for. It is the programme of Jesus Christ who died on the cross in order to bring us to peace. He is "the Way, the Truth and the Life". He will guide us into the way of peace.

To him be glory and praise for ever and ever.

+ Gabriel Zubeir Wako
Archbishop of Khartoum
President of Sudan Catholic Bishops' Conference.

VISION, MISSION AND VALUES OF THE
SUDAN CATHOLIC BISHOPS' CONFERENCE

1. PREAMBLE

We, the Catholic Bishops of the Sudan, gathered in Rome for our visit to the Tombs of the Apostles and to His Holiness the Pope, seize the occasion to hold also the Annual Plenary Assembly of our Bishops' Conference. We meditate on what should be our Mission as Bishops in the Church in the Sudan.

We reflect on our war-torn country, and on the misery, helplessness and despair of our suffering people. Christ's words to the Apostles keep ringing in our minds: "As the Father sent me, so I send you." (Jn 20:21) We feel that his Mission for us, at this moment in the history of our Church and People, can be none other than that which he gave to the Apostle, Peter: "Take care of my lambs, take care of my sheep." (Jn 21:15-16)

Sunday Mass in the southern Sudanese town of Wau, the front line of the 20 - year conflict between the government and south Sudan. In that time, about one million died in Wau and surrounding Bahr el Ghazal region.

Despite our fears and the clear awareness of our inadequacy, weakness and poverty, we repeat the commitment we made at our episcopal ordination. We will go wherever the Lord sends us. We will do whatever He commands us to do. For we know that He, true to his promise, has given us the Holy Spirit, "Receive the Holy Spirit." (Jn 20:22) He said the Spirit would remain with us always, just as He himself assured us of his presence until the end of time.

He will keep us safe and united in this work. For He prayed: "Holy Father! Keep them safe by the power of your name, the name you gave me, so that they may be one just as you and I are one." (Jn 17:11) We resolve to be living answers and witnesses to Christ's prayer by striving to live and work, united in heart and mind.

2. OUR VISION OF THE SUDAN

After the example of the Word of God who became "Emmanuel", that is "God with us", we will continue to live with our suffering people wherever they may be, to share their joy and hope, grief and anguish, until the fulfilment of the Salvation God has promised to those who place all their hope in Him. To keep their hopes and ours high and to give our aspirations a direction and our struggle a goal, we set before ourselves a "Vision of the Sudan" we would like to live in, a Sudan we must all work together to build, a Sudan that is more human.

2.1. We see and set before ourselves the vision of a Sudan in which there is:

a) No more war
b) No oppression
c) No violence
d) No tribal or ethnic hatred
e) No injustice
f) No violation of human rights
g) No discrimination because of religion

2.2 According to this vision, the Sudan should become a country in which:

a) Basic human freedoms are fully respected, defended and promoted not only by law but also in practice:
  • Freedom of conscience
  • Freedom of religion
  • Freedom of worship
  • Freedom of expression
  • Freedom of assembly
  • Freedom of movement (migration)

b) The diversity of languages, cultures and traditions is recognised, respected and valued.

c) Equal opportunity is accorded and guaranteed for each and every citizen, regardless of his/her tribe, ethnic origin, religion or gender: in other words, there should be equal opportunities:
  • For education
  • For employment
  • For access to the economic resources of the country
  • For land ownership

d) Dialogue with each other is fostered in everyday life; there is a spirit of give and take, with genuine concern for the truth and freedom from any form of fanaticism and fundamentalism.

e) A just and independent legal and judicial system is set up free from any form of political manipulation and interference, and cognisant and respectful of the diversity of cultures, customs and religious traditions that make up the Sudan.

f) Authority in Government is exercised as honest service to the people rather than as an oppressive power.

g) Leadership in whatever sphere of life is exercised transparently and with full and genuine accountability to the people.

h) Our God-given rich environmental and natural resources are respected and put to responsible use for the common good of all.

3. OUR MISSION STATEMENT

Following the example of Jesus Christ, who faithfully carried out the mission the Father entrusted to Him, we wish to adopt as our rule of life the Scriptural text that Jesus applied to himself:

> "The spirit of the Lord is upon me, because he has chosen me to bring the good news to the poor. He has sent me to proclaim liberty to captives and recovery of sight to the blind, to set free the oppressed and announce that the time has come when the Lord will save his people." (Lk 4:18-19)

In keeping with this "mission statement" of Jesus, we, the Catholic Bishops of the Sudan, make the following our pastoral priority as we strive together with our people to make our aspiration for a better and happier Sudan a tangible reality:

An aerial view of a displacement camp in Khartoum.

a) To proclaim the Good News of Salvation with renewed vigour and zeal.

b) To intensify our efforts for the on-going Christian and Spiritual formation of our people.

c) To help our people better understand the real nature of the Church and her role in society.

d) To defend and promote human dignity.

e) To stand always for justice and truth.

f) To educate and urge our faithful in the practice of peace and reconciliation.

g) To live and promote dialogue rather than confrontation with those who act and think differently from us.

h) To set up ministries that enable our people to work more effectively for their own integral human development.

i) To support the poor and needy as they struggle to change and improve their condition of life.

j) To co-operate with all people of good will in their efforts to restore justice and bring peace to our country.

4. VALUES TO SUSTAIN OUR RESOLVE

We are fully aware that the MISSION to which we are called demands continuous effort and true conversion of mind and heart. We therefore wish to keep before us certain VALUES that will permeate all we do and say, sustain us in our work, redirect our energies, and give meaning to whatever we undertake.

These are the values we shall cultivate, with God's help:

a) Faith and Trust in God who is always present to us, and who never denies us the graces we need in our lives and our work.

b) Hope in the power of Jesus' Resurrection, the guarantee that we too will triumph over death and evil.

c) Openness and Docility to the Holy Spirit who inspires and strengthens us.

Sr. Grace, from Khartoum: she said: "God gave me a heart for Africa".

d) Honesty and Truth in all circumstances.

e) Solidarity with the suffering and the needy.

f) Compassion towards the suffering and the poor just as Jesus taught us.

g) Co-operation with one another in the spirit of collegiality.

h) Reconciliation in situations of tension and conflict.

5. CONCLUSION

We renew our faith and trust in God who is faithful and mindful of his people. We let the prophet Isaiah assure us:

The LORD who created you says:
"Do not be afraid – I will save you.
I have called you by your name – you are mine.
When you pass through deep waters – I will be with you;
When you pass through fire – you will not be burnt;
The hard trials that come will not hurt you.
For I am the LORD, your God…who saves you…
Because you are precious to me.
And because I love you and give you honour.
Do not be afraid – I am with you." (Is 43:1-5)

+ Gabriel Zubeir Wako, Archbishop of Khartoum
+ Paulino Lukundu Loro, Archbishop of Juba
+ Joseph Gasi Abanjite, Bishop of Tambura-Yambio
+ Vincent Mojwok Nyiker, Bishop of Malakal
+ Paride Taban, Bishop of Torit
+ Makram Max Gassis, Bishop of El Obeid
+ Erkolano Lado Tombe, Bishop of Yei
+ Antonio Menegazzo, Administrator Apostolic of El Obeid
+ Daniel Adowk Kur, Auxiliary Bishop of Khartoum
Msgr Cesar Mazzolari, Administrator Apostolic of Rumbek

FORGIVE AND YOU WILL BE FORGIVEN
THE COMMON GOOD IS THE SUPREME LAW
February 2003
Marking 10 years since the Pope's visit to Sudan

Memories of the Pope's visit to Sudan remained vivid in the imagination of the faithful who saw him that February day in 1993 when he celebrated Mass in Khartoum's Green Square. Soon after, the optimism, which his visit had ushered in, quickly vanished as the war in the south became still worse. Then in 2002, as talks got underway in Machakos, central Kenya, glimmers of hope began to emerge in the discussions between the Government of Sudan and the rebels. In a letter marking the 10th anniversary of the Pope's visit, Archbishop Zubeir Wako flags up hopes of peace to a people desperate for an end to war.

Dear Brothers and Sisters,

We are writing to you remembering the joyful occasion of the tenth anniversary of the official and historic visit of His Holiness Pope John Paul II to the Sudan. We also celebrate the tenth anniversary of the Beatification of St Josephine Bakhita, already declared a saint during the Great Jubilee of the Year 2000.

On that occasion many good wishes for peace and prosperity had been exchanged between H.H. the Pope and H.E. the President of the Sudan, Omar al Bashir. The Pope, at that time, declared that he was happy to visit the Sudan and to offer to all the Sudanese people – irrespective of differences of religion and ethnic origin – a message of reconciliation and hope.

The immense sufferings of innocent victims urged him to voice his solidarity with the weak and defenceless and cry out to God for help, justice and respect for their dignity, human rights, for freedom to embrace and practise their faith without fear of discrimination.

The President Omar al Bashir, on the same occasion, confirmed: "God Himself has already and unequivocally stated in the Koran that there shall be no compulsion in matters of faith. Muslim Jurists and Scholars throughout the ages have unanimously held that compulsion in matters of faith is not only void but also a sin and a crime punishable by the Shari'a Law."

The Pope therefore foresaw the beginning of a "new relationship" between Christians and Muslims, that would reverse the policy of hatred and discrimination in this land, as stated by the President in his welcoming speech at the airport. "We are confident that our combined efforts and the efforts of all men of good will, will enable us to achieve these cherished objectives and Sudan will once again become a land of peace, tolerance and spiritual values as it has been always throughout history."

Unfortunately, after ten years, we realise that these words of good wishes have vanished in the war's winds! Only in the last few months our hope was raised on hearing some serious attempts towards peace are going on in Kenya at the Machakos Peace Talks.

The immense suffering of innocent victims urged the Pope to voice his solidarity with the weak and defenceless

St. Matthew's Cathedral, Khartoum. seat of Cardinal Gabriel

The Lesson of St Josephine Bakhita

As we all know, Josephine was cruelly taken into slavery as a child, violently uprooted from her family, deprived of her indispensable cradle of love to be plunged forcibly into a situation of slavery and terror. Indeed she had all natural reasons to hate her torturers, to nurture revenge against her persecutors who destroyed her future, selling her as a commodity for material gain.

But the Lord has been great with Josephine! He worked a marvel in her life through the Spirit of the Lord Jesus Christ, to the point that she was able to say: "If I could meet those who uprooted me from my home, I would kiss their hands."

In her life long spiritual journey of prayer, charity and humility, she achieved the grace of utter forgiveness for her offenders, of totally acknowledging that God has been able to draw good from evil in her life and transform the crime of her persecutors into a unique opportunity of coming to know Christ.
She stands before us and the world as an heroic model of that form of love which is forgiveness. She showed herself to be a true disciple of Jesus, who at the moment of death, prayed the Father to forgive his murderers.

"No peace without justice, no justice without forgiveness"

Often we may think that justice and forgiveness are irreconcilable. "Forgiveness is in no way opposed to justice as if to forgive meant to overlook the need to right the wrong done. It is rather the fullness of justice, leading to that tranquillity of order which is much more than a fragile and temporary cessation of hostilities, involving as it does the deepest healing of the wounds which fester in human hearts. Justice and forgiveness are both essential to such healing." (John Paul II, January 1, 2002).

We may just imagine what a hell of bitterness could have been the life of St Josephine Bakhita if she had not forgiven those who ravaged her life so cruelly! She would never have been the model of serenity and peace of heart and mind, which in fact everyone recognises in her gentle image.

What about justice? St Bakhita in no way condoned the slavery with her forgiveness: on the contrary, she has become a living strong denunciation of the brutality of slavery, in front of all the world and for time to come. She unequivocally condemned the evil by her very flesh, slowly developing with the Spirit of the Lord an unconditional forgiveness for the evil-doers. The path of forgiveness is the path of the followers of Christ, a path, which has a divine source and criterion, but can also be grasped in the light of human reasoning.

"Forgiveness is above all a personal choice, but it has a special dimension. Families, groups, societies, States and the international community need forgiveness in order to renew ties that have been set asunder, go beyond sterile situations of natural condemnation and overcome the temptation to discriminate against others without appeal. The ability to forgive lies at the very basis of the idea of a future society marked by justice and solidarity. Forgiveness is necessary for development; a failure to forgive often prolongs conflict. National resources are wasted on weapons, suffering is inflicted because of failure to reconcile." (John Paul II)

Financial resources for peace, never for war!

To promote effectively these ways of peace and prosperity, the massive financial daily income of this country needs to be positively channelled with determination. God has been so generous with Sudan in providing us with such huge wealth! We are accountable to Him for the good use of it. We need to direct it in order to promote a culture of life, justice and peace. In particular, to squander these gratuitous gifts in trading weapons of devastation and death, would constitute a tremendous responsibility in front of Him, the people.

We need to put all our efforts together in order to wage the urgent war against poverty, ignorance, hunger and disease.

The Paschal mystery and prayer

The life of St Bakhita shows us how her union with the mystery of the death and resurrection of Jesus and the power of prayer, had the power to transform the calamity of her life in an extraordinary blessing for her and for the world. She was able to accept with faith and peace what would normally appear unbearable to any person even less fragile than her. Without prayer, such a miracle would be unimaginable.

Also for each one of us the possibility to unite ourselves with the Paschal Mystery (passion, death and resurrection of the Lord) and to resort to prayer at any time, is at hand today.

May St Bakhita help us to continue with determination and faith working for justice, peace and reconciliation, even though this will not be achieved without tribulations and suffering.

As we close, we cannot fail to point out that as we celebrate the 10th anniversary of St Bakhita, we do so in the year 2003 when

Bishop Daniel Comboni is being canonised (October 5th 2003).
These two Saints belong par excellence to the people of Sudan,
and complement each other in presenting to the Church of Sudan
and the Church at large the need of total regeneration for the
people of Sudan and many unspoken of people in our world.
Human dignity, freedom and full entry of the global reality of
today's world socially, economically and ecclesially must be brought
about through the genuine declaration of a truly missionary
Church, an unselfish reaching out of brothers and sisters in mutual
solidarity and the strong commitment to enable one another to
develop, share and enjoy the spiritual and material value of our
God-given creation here and hereafter.

May the Lord bless you.

+ Gabriel Zubeir Wako
Archbishop of Khartoum

FROM A SITUATION OF CHAOS
TO A COUNTRY OF PEACE
Letter from Cardinal Gabriel Zubeir Wako to
Omar al Bashir, The President of Sudan
27 May, 2004

*On May 26th 2004, the Government of Sudan and the rebel Sudanese
People's Liberation Army/Movement (SPLA/M) signed an historic
declaration of peace in Naivasha, Kenya. The settlement ended 20 years of
war in which at least two million died and more than five million have
fled their homes. As the two sides took the historic step to agree to share
power and oil revenues, attention began to focus on the prospects for a
referendum six years on, when the South will be able to vote on
independence from the North. To have got this far was a tribute to the
Cardinal's unrelenting struggle for peace. But the media frenzy over Darfur
and the clear signs of Government implication gave rise to speculation that
the Government of Sudan had only brokered peace in the south to buy
time for the campaign in the west.*

Your Excellency,

The Peace of God be with you and all the Sudanese People.

I send you this message in order to congratulate you and express
my appreciation for the Protocols for Peace signed in Naivasha. I
thank you that, under your leadership, the Sudanese People can
now truly hope to live together in peace, harmony and
brotherliness. The process, if continued, promises great blessings for
the Sudan. It is a great blessing of God that He put into your heart
and in that of those you formerly considered rebels to work

together in search of a way out of war into real peace. It is my hope, and the hope of every one who has the good of our country truly at heart, that we consider the step taken in Naivasha a step into a journey with no return.

May the country now embark on the project of building a "new" Sudan - the kind of Sudan in which violence, injustice, discrimination find no place, because people's hearts and minds have been filled with all that brings and holds them together.

I pray that the Lord may lead the Sudanese People on to the final signing of the Peace Agreement, and that nothing political, religious, social or economic may ever be done to lead this People back into armed conflicts and the unnecessary shedding of blood.

Finally, I declare my readiness as well as duty to work together with you and all people of good will in strengthening the process of peace. The Catholic Bishops of the Sudan have expressed this same readiness time and again in the past. You can therefore count on our cooperation in all that will help strengthen peace in our country and reverse the evil of the many years of war.

May God bless you and all who work closely with you in raising the Sudan from a situation of chaos into a country of Peace and Progress.

+ Gabriel Cardinal Zubeir Wako
Archbishop of Khartoum

Khartoum's Christian displacement camps spreading out as far as the eye can see.

Enjoying the personal backing of the Pope, Aid to the Church in Need is a registered charity dedicated to the support of persecuted and oppressed Christians. Central to ACN's mission is to bring Christ to the world.

Aid to the Church in Need was founded by the Dutch Norbertine priest Fr Werenfried van Straaten O. Praem.

A genius fund-raiser, Fr Werenfried's pioneering work began in 1947 offering material and spiritual help to refugees in Germany. Earning the title "Bacon Priest", Fr Werenfried provided food and blankets and soon set about launching initiatives such as "Chapel trucks" for suffering faithful in search of a Mass to attend.

Fr Werenfried's early success emboldened him to expand his charity and in a few years he was supporting Christians suffering for their faith behind the Iron Curtain.

Dressed in a disguise, including a false moustache, he offered key assistance to prelates and people such as the embattled Hungarian Primate, Cardinal Mindszenty and Polish Primate Cardinal Wyszynski.

At the specific request of Pope John XXIII, Father Werenfried widened the scope of his work still further when in the early 1960s he led his charity to start helping beleaguered Christians in Latin America. Soon after, his work spread to Africa.

When he died in 2003, Pope John Paul II named him an "Outstanding Apostle of Charity". The charity - whose UK office is in Sutton, Surrey - now undertakes thousands of projects every year. The organisation is now at work in about 130 countries throughout the world.

Aid to the Church in Need supports...

• More than 16,000 seminarians worldwide. They receive books and buildings essential to their progress to the Altar of God.

• Many thousands of nuns. The charity helps nuns in Eastern Europe with everything from training for novices to centres for pastoral work.

• Countless priests who receive Aid to the Church in Need Mass stipends. The money provides a roof over their head and basic food and warmth.

• The construction of churches and other essential church buildings

• Clergy and catechists with basic transport to minister to their flock. Everything from boats to bicycles, motorbikes to mules are the gift of ACN to the clergy.

• Young people who receive ACN's Child's Bibles. Since the initiative was launched more than 25 years ago, more than over 40 million have gone out in over 140 languages.

Sudan is Aid to the Church in Need's "priority country" in Africa. In 2004 the charity launched an international campaign to support the suffering Church there, especially diocesan schools, programmes of spiritual and pastoral renewal in destitute areas, training for priests, seminarians and catechists and support for refugees in the disaster-stricken crisis in the western region of Darfur.